Ariadne's Thread

Awakening the Wonders of the Ancient Minoans in our Modern Lives

Ariadne's Thread

Awakening the Wonders of
the Ancient Minoans in our
Modern Lives

Laura Perry

Winchester, UK
Washington, USA

First published by Moon Books, 2013
Moon Books is an imprint of John Hunt Publishing Ltd., Laurel House, Station Approach,
Alresford, Hants, SO24 9JH, UK
office1@jhpbooks.net
www.johnhuntpublishing.com
www.moon-books.net

For distributor details and how to order please visit the 'Ordering' section on our website.

Text copyright: Laura Perry 2013

ISBN: 978 1 78279 110 2

A CIP catalogue record for this book is available from the British Library.

Design: Stuart Davies

Printed and bound by CPI Group (UK) Ltd, Croydon, CR0 4YY

We operate a distinctive and ethical publishing philosophy in all
areas of our business, from our global network of authors to
production and worldwide distribution.

CONTENTS

List of Illustrations

Preface

When I was 14, my art teacher showed my class photos of the frescoes from the walls of the palace at Knossos and the halls of Thera. Of course, I thought they were beautiful – all those vivid colors and naturalistic figures – but something about them tickled a hidden spot in the back of my psyche, and in all the years since then I've continued to be entranced by the people and culture of ancient Crete.

As I grew to adulthood and went through the demanding process of defining my beliefs and spirituality, I realized that much of the ancient world held values and attitudes that matched mine. Among them, the marvelous Minoans.

Since then I have been happily reading and researching about Minoan history, culture and spirituality. As a solitary practitioner and in groups large and small, I have enacted the rituals in this book, to honor the deities and energies of ancient Crete. I offer my thanks to the friends, covens and groves who have worked these ceremonies with me, reveling in the vitality of this beautiful culture and celebrating its deities and ideals.

The balance between the masculine and feminine, a primary component of Minoan spirituality, brings a vital value to our modern world as we grapple with issues of equality and acceptance. Here there are no forbidding gods of force and threat, no power-hungry deities who demand blind obedience, just a loving mother and her family, ready to surround us with their embrace.

Introduction

Ancient Crete was a magical place filled with the power of living myth and the richness of a culture whose roots extended back into the dim mists of prehistory. Recall the legend of the young hero Theseus who set out to slay the dreadful half-man, half-bull Minotaur in the labyrinth at Knossos. Through the grace of the goddess Ariadne (depicted as a maiden or princess in most versions of the tale) Theseus not only found his way to the center of the labyrinth, but following her thread, he found his way out again to freedom and safety.

This same tradition brings us the myth of the bull-god Zagreus, later known as Dionysus, who suckled at the breast of the goat-goddess Amalthea in the sacred cave on Mount Dikte. The legends and artwork of ancient Crete tell of griffins and fauns, sphinxes and naiads adventuring across this small island in the Mediterranean Sea and interacting with humans and deities alike.

The myths of ancient Crete, her people, and their gods twine through our minds like the snakes around the priestess' arms in those ancient temples. They call to us across the millennia, asking us to remember. In answer to that call, *Ariadne's Thread* focuses on honoring Crete's magic, touching its power, and commemorating the richness of a world in which women and men worked and worshiped as equals. In these pages, the glory of Crete once again springs to life – the history, the culture, and most of all, the intense spirituality that can inspire and transform our modern ways of thinking, worshiping and being. The ruined temples and mansions of ancient Crete may crumble along the coastline of this tiny island, but Ariadne's thread still leads us into the labyrinth and safely back out again.

The ruins that still stand on Crete today hint at a glory and greatness we can only imagine. Those expansive temples, colorful frescoes, and intricate mosaics are the remnants of a highly developed culture whose religion and way of life offer us much food for thought. These were a powerful, peaceful people. They lived as they believed, with equality between women and men, an active and free international market and a reverence for the Earth that bore them all.

Some of the ideas in this book are at odds with the way we have often been taught to envision Ariadne and her island. Sir Arthur Evans' excavations at the turn of the 20th century and his interpretation of the artifacts he found have profoundly colored our view of Minoan culture. Evans' chauvinistic Victorian mindset encouraged him to depict ancient Crete as a male-dominated mercantile society ruled by a powerful male monarchy. This view is far from the truth. Fortunately, archaeologists such as Nanno Marinatos and scholars such as Riane Eisler have uncovered and shared with us the wonders of the egalitarian society that carried Crete to such heights of culture and spirituality. Though it was no utopia, this ancient culture has much to teach us about how to live in equality and peace.

Women and men alike participated in ancient Crete's flourishing economy, running businesses and trading with merchants from around the world. The inhabitants of the island enjoyed a safe, clean living environment that would be the envy of any modern city. And the monarchy that Evans envisioned ruling over the island and its vast wealth never existed. Crete's economy and culture flourished under the guidance of a class of priestesses and priests who directed the seasonal activities of the cities from the temples they served. Over all the merchants, the priestesses and priests, over all the cities with their beautiful temples, over all of Crete rose the goddess Ariadne, guiding and blessing these fascinating people. From her tale, and from the example of the ancient Minoans, we can draw wisdom and guidance to improve the world we live in today.

From the earliest settlements to the fall of the last temples, the inhabitants of Crete honored their goddesses and gods in their own way. They prized the balance of feminine and masculine, the complementary halves that make the cosmic Whole. And they had a special place in their hearts and their lives for Ariadne, the Weaver of Life. The society that developed on Crete honored the goddess as the source of all existence. As we of the modern world rediscover the feminine in the divine, we can draw inspiration and power from the Great Goddess as the ancients knew her.

The pages that follow introduce a cycle of rituals that draw on the energies and history of the people of this fascinating island. These rites include new and full moon ceremonies for magical workings, seasonal festivals to celebrate the turning of the year, and rites of passage to acknowledge the turning points in our lives. You will find details about the many deities of ancient Crete and their sacred symbols in a separate chapter about the Minoan pantheon. Anywhere you come across a god or goddess name in **bold type**, this indicates that you can find more information about that deity in the chapter about the pantheon.

Crete's goddesses and gods live on in the hearts and minds of all who are open to them, and the rituals have a great deal of relevance for those of us today who seek respect, equality and balance in the modern world.

May Ariadne lead you to your own special thread in the labyrinth of life.

Part One

Work, Play and Worship in Ancient Crete

Chapter 1

A Brief History of Crete

For having made such a great impression on the ancient world, Crete is remarkably small. The island itself is only 150 miles long and barely 20 miles wide, resting in the blue-green Mediterranean Sea just southeast of Greece. It is almost equally distant from Europe, Asia and Africa, an ideal position from which to wield social as well as economic influence in the ancient world. The island is dramatic to behold. The rocky beaches and lowlands turn sharply upward toward a steep and craggy central mountain range. These sacred mountains reach an incredible 8,000 feet in altitude at their height, a truly spectacular home for Crete's goddesses and gods.

Although the mountainous highlands are too barren to plow and can only be used to graze sheep and goats, the area around the perimeter of the island has always been fertile, if somewhat rocky. The lowlands were heavily wooded at the height of Crete's glory (2000-1500 BCE) but have unfortunately been cleared in recent times. The temperate climate with its hot summers, mild winters and a constant sea breeze has long been responsible for the abundance of such traditional Mediterranean crops as grains, olives, beans and grapes. Since Crete is an island, it has its share of fog, damp and mist, but only high in the mountains does the wind come sharp and frigid in the winter.

Many people refer to those who lived on Crete in ancient times as Minoans. This name is derived from the title of the Minos, the bull-king or bull-god priest who presided at the temple at Knossos. Technically, the term *Minoan* refers only to the Bronze Age culture on Crete, from approximately the 27th to the 15th century BCE. But since it is such a well-known term, and since the word *Cretan* is often confused with the derogatory *cretin*, I will use *Minoan* in reference to the ancient people and their culture across the centuries.

Though archaeologists have found traces of early hominids dating back 130,000 years in southern Crete, most scholars agree that human settlement did not occur until about 9,000 years ago, in the Late Stone Age. These early farmers and herders probably came across the Mediterranean from Asia Minor. First they settled along the eastern tip of Crete, then slowly expanded westward over the island. They built small houses of stone or wattle-and-daub, and buried their dead in caves.

By 2,000 years later (about 5000 BCE), the islanders were practicing advanced agriculture and expanding their settlements. Over the following three millennia they developed a complex society with villages and towns populated by artisans, farmers and merchants.

By the beginning of the Bronze Age, about 3000 BCE, the Minoans had regular trade contact with the Cycladic Islands and Egypt. They built tombs rather than bury their dead in caves. And they began the creation of one of the most successful cultures in the ancient world.

For the next 2,000 years they flourished, building a society based not on military conquest but on mercantile activities. They traded the wares of their own talented artists and craftspeople as well as items they brought back from foreign lands. Minoan goods such as colorful painted pottery, delicate jewelry, carved stone vases and ornate jeweled daggers were popular with merchants throughout the known world.

From the time of the earliest European civilization, Crete was a trade center not only for Europe but also for the Middle East and other areas as well. The Minoans traded closely with Egypt for centuries; Egyptian influence is evident in Minoan art and architecture. In fact, the artisans and merchants from Crete shipped their goods as far away as Spain. They traded and established colonies in Asia Minor and southern Palestine, including the town of Gaza, whose earlier name was Minoa.

On Crete itself four port towns along the north and east coasts of the island grew large and rich enough to become known throughout the ancient world. Crowned with expansive temples, these cities were the strength and glory of Minoan civilization. From Knossos and Malia on the north coast around to Zakros in the east and Phaistos in the south, they provided a focus for the flow of goods and wealth that gave the Minoans their lavish lifestyle. Each city ruled itself and the surrounding farmland, but they remained independent from each other, much like the later Greek city-states.

The people of Crete had their own writing systems, an earlier hieroglyphic script and a later syllabary called Linear A. We still do not understand the language that it symbolized, though many people have attempted to decipher it.

Nature herself appears to have caused the downfall of Minoan society. During the 17th century BCE the volcanic island of Thera (modern Santorini) in the eastern Mediterranean exploded violently. The resulting earthquakes, tidal wave and ash fallout did extensive damage to Crete and some buildings were abandoned at that time.

The Minoans managed to rebuild many of their most important structures, including the temples at Knossos, Phaistos and Malia. In fact, the new buildings grew to a far grander scale than the original ones. But just two centuries later another natural disaster occurred and all the temples except the one at Knossos were either abandoned or destroyed. Archaeologists and historians still argue over the exact nature of the catastrophe that occurred at that time, but general consensus leans toward another volcanic eruption with its attendant earthquake, tidal wave, ash cloud and resulting fires and crop failures.

Knossos remained a center of religious and economic activity for about a century after the widespread collapse, but during this time large numbers of mainland Greeks (Mycenaeans) immigrated to Crete. They introduced their own language and modified the Minoan Linear A script into Linear B to use for writing Mycenaean Greek. Under the influence of the Greeks and their foreign, male-dominated culture, by the 12th century BCE Minoan society had effectively ceased to exist.

Through this vast expanse of time, the population on Crete grew from a few small settlements to a network of sprawling towns. Minoan religious centers grew from a few scattered tombs and sanctuaries to a network of highly organized, complex temples, only to fall prey to the power of Mother Nature in the end. Now that we know something of their history, let's explore the culture and religious practices of this fascinating ancient people.

Chapter 2

Daily Life in Ancient Crete

Two Sides of One Coin

We know from the archaeological record that the grand Minoan 'palaces' functioned as temples, housing the priestly class and providing a setting for rituals and ceremonies. But the temples had another function as well, one we tend to forget from our vantage point in a separation-of-church-and-state society. The temples also played a major role in the economic and political life of ancient Crete. We modern folk tend to think of people and institutions as belonging to either the religious sector of society or the economic/industrial sector but not both. On Crete, however, religion and commerce were intertwined to the point that we often cannot discern the boundaries. This was a common situation in the ancient world.

The priestly class, both women and men, who lived in the temples, wielded a great amount of power in Crete's society. The wealthy merchants who lived around the temples also exerted a certain amount of influence. For the Minoans, religion was an integral part of their daily lives. Craftsmen performed rituals in the process of creating their products. Most ordinary houses included shrines and altars. Grand public ceremonies and rituals displayed the Minoans' wealth to visiting merchants, further encouraging trade. Although we cannot call ancient Crete a full theocracy, since as far as we know the priestly class was not the sole ruling group on the island, there is truly no way to separate religion from any other aspect of life there.

How did so many facets of Minoan society and daily life revolve around the temples? First of all, we are well-acquainted with the temples' use as grain storage sites, a common function of religious centers in the ancient world. From the early granaries situated alongside the ceremonial courts to the later storage rooms filled with pottery jars of grain as tall as a robust adult, the temples were a repository for the island's surplus grain supply.

It is possible that this excess was saved for ritual feasting, although some of it was certainly held back as insurance in case of famine, as was common in the ancient world. The grain storage areas in the temples, as well as in some of the surrounding mansions, are full of ritual artwork and symbology. We find religious symbols such as double axes and Linear A writing on the walls of the storerooms. A number of the storage areas also encompass shrines or lead directly to shrine or ritual areas. Thus we can imagine a ritual blessing or protection of this basic foodstuff, either when it was first stockpiled or as it was later distributed to buyers or ritual participants.

The temples also provided workspace for artists and crafts-people who produced jewelry, pottery, sculpture, paintings and many other fine wares. Some of the most intricately worked, valuable pieces of jewelry and pottery have been found in the shrines, sanctuaries and public areas of the temple complexes. It is probable that temple-produced goods commanded a high price due to their association with the sacred center. Of course, many artisans also lived and worked in the towns, selling their wares in the lively, well-traveled markets. But it must have been quite an honor to earn a place in the workrooms of one of the temples.

There is one aspect of the Minoan temples which is not obvious at first, perhaps because it is characterized by the absence of something rather than its presence. Unlike so many of the great religious complexes built by other ancient civilizations, the temples on Crete were not monuments to any particular rulers or leaders. We find no portraits of kings, or queens for that matter. We find no lists of battles won or conquests made, no depictions of conquered peoples being enslaved or killed. The

Minoan temples are remarkably bare of depictions of violence or domination of any kind.

The temples, in fact, appear to have been built with aesthetic rather than monumental purposes in mind. They were designed for the worship of the deities and ancestors of this world, to reinforce the connection between the human and the divine. And, unlike the Christian cathedrals which sought to dwarf and intimidate people and make them feel inferior to the great Christian God, the Minoan temples sought to draw people into the order of being and make them feel a part of the divine that surrounded and penetrated them.

Life in Town

When we talk about ancient Crete we often focus on the temples due to their imposing presence and architectural beauty. But we must remember that most of the Minoan population lived outside the temple grounds, in the towns and nearby farming areas. Their lives would not be as foreign to us as we might think.

The developed areas of Crete ringed the eastern half of the coastline, with the towns sloping up from low-lying harbors towards the villas and temples. We often think of wealthy ancient civilizations in terms of highly stratified societies such as Egypt and Rome. In those empires, though the upper echelons enjoyed great wealth and luxury, the poorer people labored long and hard in subhuman living conditions. Crete, however, grew out of a different paradigm. The Minoans, more than perhaps any other early society, shared the accumulated wealth of their trading empire among all the island's inhabitants. Yes, there were poor people and there were vastly rich people, but even the poorest Minoans still lived in a clean, relatively safe environment along paved, well-drained streets.

The poorest families lived near the harbors in simple, small plaster houses built close together. These houses often had only one main room, with little furniture and few cooking implements.

Built along a design familiar to modern Americans from the pioneer days, these houses included a sleeping loft above the main living area. Though the people who lived in these houses were poor, they had plenty of food from the island's harbors. They had a clean supply of water from town cisterns and viaducts and they lived in what was likely the safest of the ancient civilizations, street crime being largely unknown on the island.

The people who lived down by the harbors were the manual labor so necessary for Crete's vast trade empire. These people carried merchandise from the many ships up to the markets, cared for the merchants' pack animals, and occasionally sold trade goods themselves. They were probably not literate, for only those who could afford temple schooling or private tutors learned to read and write.

In contrast to the illiterate manual laborers, some Minoans could afford to pay for schooling. These were the more successful merchants and artisans who lived farther into the towns, away from the harbors (and the smell of fish). These people held jobs we would probably find familiar. Some of them were traders and merchants who had permanent shops or stalls in the marketplaces. They traded in foodstuffs from nearby and faraway lands – dates, fruit, wines, nuts. They bought and sold the basic necessities as well as the luxuries the Minoans so desired. Through the harbors and marketplaces of ancient Crete flowed shipments of cooking pots and dishes, decorative pottery, lumber, perfume oil, raw gold, silver and precious stones, tools for woodworking and metalsmithing, in short, many of the sorts of things we buy and sell in our world today.

Let us not forget the rural islanders who lived in the foothills of the jagged central mountain range. These people farmed the rocky soil, producing the staple foods of Minoan society. They also herded goats and sheep, animals that can easily adapt to rugged, mountainous terrain. The crops, the animals and the people all benefited from the extensive irrigation system whose canals carried water across the island's farmlands.

One class of people we would not find in ancient Crete is the military. Crete had no army or navy of its own and, until the Mycenaean incursions toward the end of the empire, did not hire mercenaries or guards from other lands. The Minoans preferred to concentrate their energies and capital on trade rather than warfare. They wanted no land other than their own small island and thus posed no threat to the surrounding nations.

One interesting outgrowth of this lack of military is a sort of warrior cult that grew up among the young men of Crete. Having no other outlet for their competitive or aggressive energy, they developed a subculture within Minoan society. These young men participated in ritualized displays of hunting skill, flaunting their prowess with weapons such as the spear and dagger. They often included hunting forays as part of initiation rituals, proving their manliness by their skill with their chosen weapons.

This subsection of Minoan culture looked to the young god as their role model. They depicted him as a muscular, handsome youth who carried a tall spear and wore a dagger at his belt. The young men who worshiped this god often wore ornately decorated daggers as part of their dress as well, emphasizing their economic and spiritual stature with such weapons. Interestingly enough, though, the young men of Crete limited their aggression to the animals they hunted rather than warring on each other or neighboring peoples.

The Minoans had no centralized government. Each town ruled itself through the guidance of the priestly class and the wealthiest merchants. There was enough trade and wealth flowing through the harbors of Crete that the towns' inhabitants had no desire to take over anyone else's territory. By concentrating on the flow of trade rather than spending money on a destructive and unnecessary military, the Minoans built up the strongest, farthest-reaching mercantile empire of the classical world.

Many of the raw materials that were shipped into Crete's harbors made their way to the island's artisans. By the time of the great temples and the height of Crete's renown, the island was heavily populated with expert architects, engineers, engravers, weavers, metalsmiths, fresco painters, faience workers, potters and all manner of other artisans. They ran a thriving trade in everything from the most expensive, precious handmade items commissioned by the rich merchants and temple residents to mass-produced commercial jewelry and cooking pots. Their metalsmiths worked copper, bronze, silver and gold, fashioning it into jewelry, decorative containers, knives and daggers. Minoan potters crafted vases, jugs, bowls and cups of fine ceramic, intricately painted with beautiful, brightly colored scenes and designs.

While some of the consumer goods produced on Crete were shipped around the Mediterranean in trade, the Minoans themselves bought much of what their artisans produced. This 'middle class' on Crete, the successful merchants and crafts-people, lived in multi-room houses set along wide paved streets. Even by our standards they lived well; many of their houses were equipped with beautifully decorated terracotta bathtubs. Like many European houses today, the fronts of the houses were close to the street and the box or horseshoe shape of the buildings enclosed private, beautifully landscaped courtyards. In these courtyards the Minoans strolled, relaxed, and ate their meals when the weather was pleasant, which it was for much of the year. They spent a good deal of time outdoors or on open verandahs, taking advantage of the mild climate.

The foods they ate in ancient times are remarkably similar to what the people around the Mediterranean eat today. The ancient Minoans enjoyed goat, mutton and pork, all raised domestically, as well as many varieties of wild game. Of course, the island's coastline provided an abundance of fresh fish and shellfish. This bounty from the sea was the primary food of the poor people who lived along the harbors, but it was also a favorite of the rest of the island's inhabitants. Minoan farmers raised domesticated sheep and goats on farms outside the towns. These animals provided milk and cheese as well as meat for the dinner table.

We often think of kitchens in ancient times as centering around a large firepit or fireplace. The Minoans, however, did not build chimneys into their houses, perhaps due to the warm climate. Instead they did most of their cooking over a portable charcoal brazier set on the floor or, occasionally, on a table. They grilled meat directly on the brazier much as we would do at a barbecue. For other foods they used copper or mixed metal cookpots on top of the brazier. They even managed to bake wheat and barley bread this way. While they apparently knew about yeast for leavening, it was not widely available, so the majority of their bread was unleavened. From the countryside they brought in honey to sweeten their food, though this was a luxury available only to those who could afford it.

The island's moderate climate allowed for the cultivation of a number of different fruits and those that could not be grown on Crete were imported from other lands. Thus the Minoans enjoyed a wide variety of fruit, both fresh and cooked or preserved, including pears, quinces, grapes, pomegranates, figs and dates. To serve and eat this wide variety of foods they used dishes and utensils which look startlingly familiar – teacups and wine goblets, bowls, wine jugs, and pottery storage jars. In all, their culinary life was not much different from what the people in that region enjoy today.

A small but important segment of Minoan society was the musicians. The people of Crete considered music to be a very important part of life and held musicians in high regard. The temple-dwellers and wealthy merchants often hired musicians to play for them as they went about their daily activities as well as at feasts and celebrations. We also know that music was an important part of their rituals and ceremonies. Minoan musicians played a range of instruments including the zither, lyre-harp, double-pipe flute and drums. Often, musicians played together as an ensemble to entertain the guests at parties and feasts. In fact the zither, a string instrument similar to the later European dulcimer, was invented on Crete. We have record of Minoans singing and dancing as a musician plays a sistrum, a rattle-like instrument of Egyptian origin. And, in much the same way that modern Greeks perform folk dances, the Minoans danced in circles with arms linked.

High Style

For most people, the term Minoan conjures up an image of heavily made-up, finely dressed and bejeweled men and women. While this may be an accurate picture of the wealthy upper classes and the priesthood at the height of Crete's glory, the majority of the population wore the same sorts of clothes that the locals had been wearing for centuries.

The working classes wore either simple tunics, sometimes belted, or chitons, a loosely gathered garment also worn by the mainland Greeks, all made of coarse wool or linen. The men often wore simple knee-length wrap skirts, tied or belted at the waist. In the balmy island climate many men went bare-chested, and laborers in the harbor or on board merchant ships might wear nothing but a loincloth. The ordinary people had little selection for footwear – simple leather sandals or boots were all that was available. Even the well-to-do craftsmen wore simple, sturdy clothes when they worked, for obvious reasons. The upper classes, however, had a much greater variety to choose from.

Those whose work did not involve physical labor dressed in fine linen, often woven with metallic threads or hand-printed with floral or geometric designs. The women's dresses hung to the ankles and it was quite fashionable to layer several skirts of different lengths together with the hems hanging one above the other. The women's tops were open down the front and could be worn with the edges together for a modest look or with the front wide open, revealing the breasts. To complete the stylish Minoan ensemble, the women wore tight corset-like girdles (wide belts) at the waist.

Minoan art depicts narrow waists as fashionable for both women and men so the men often wore tight belts or girdles as well. But the men's garments were based around a gathered or pleated knee-length skirt, sometimes referred to as a kilt. Like their working-class counterparts, wealthy Minoan men often went without a shirt, the climate being warm for a good part of the year. Like the women of their island, the men wore their hair long and carefully styled into braids or ringlets.

One striking aspect of Minoan fashion is its emphasis on sexuality. This should not be surprising coming from a society that found no sin or guilt in sexual display and activity. The people of ancient Crete celebrated their bodies just as they celebrated their beautiful island home and their gods. The women's clothing often emphasized bare breasts. The men's clothing could be quite scanty, often consisting of nothing more than a very short skirt and sandals. Minoan men also wore a close-fitting garment much like modern bicycle shorts, made of fabric cut on the bias for stretch. In addition, the men wore exaggerated codpieces on the fronts of their skirts much like the ones that Renaissance European men sported.

Both men and women displayed their wealth through intricately woven trims and ribbons on their clothing, heavy makeup, and expensive jewelry. The men also wore ornate daggers, often with jeweled hilts, to display their high status. Such weapons were a (sometimes ostentatious) display of wealth. While the women usually wore sandals, the men often wore soft leather boots, but all were made of high quality leather and sometimes gilded or decorated with jewels. Those who stayed indoors often went without shoes, a mark of extreme luxury.

North Wing of Knossos Temple, the Grandstand Fresco

Artistic depictions of the different classes of Minoan society on frescoes and pottery show the priestly class wearing distinctive garb. We are familiar with the beautifully-dressed snake priestesses with their flounced skirts, embroidered aprons and tight girdles. But these garments were also worn by well-to-do people outside the temples. The distinction between ordinary women and priestesses, when they were otherwise dressed alike, is the headgear worn only by the clergy. Minoan priestesses wore headbands, hats and coronets as a symbol of their office. Headdresses adorned with lilies are a particular attribute of priestesses and also of the Minoan version of that female mythological creature, the sphinx.

Another piece of distinctive costuming that sets the priesthood apart is skirts made of animal hide. These above-ankle-length garments were worn by the men and the women of the priestly class, with or without a top. Hide skirts were a particular mark of the clergy who performed animal sacrifice rituals. The animal skins they wore linked them with the energy of the animal that was ritually sacrificed to the gods and shared with them as food.

The item of distinctive garb that set the male priests apart from other Minoans was their ankle-length robe, in contrast to the common short kilt and girdle. These priestly robes were decorated with diagonal bands of embroidery or ribbon, often ending in tassels. Minoan priests depicted in frescoes and on seal-stones also sported a characteristic hairstyle. These images show the men with short bangs in the front and shoulder-length hair in the back. They also wore beards, a fashion uncommon among those outside the priesthood.

Chapter 3

Minoan Spirituality:
From Caves to Temples to Caves

In the Beginning...

Our earliest glimpse of Minoan religion comes not from the houses and settlements of the people on the island, but from their tombs and burial sites. Before there were even towns on Crete, while the people still lived in loose settlements along the eastern and southern coast, they began erecting tombs. These funerary buildings varied in size and shape from region to region and were the Minoans' largest mark on their tiny island until the time of the great temples.

These numerous tombs formed a focal point for funerary rites and possibly a cult of the dead during the early to mid-third millennium BCE. Some of them were carved into the rocks that faced the sea, becoming man-made caves. Others were constructed of stone, large circular buildings with smaller rectangular rooms added on around the edges. Located imposingly on the flat plains of eastern and southern Crete, these tombs were filled with valuable items, often crafted of gold or ivory, that were placed among the multiple burials as funeral gifts. Among the burial gifts that archaeologists have unearthed are jewelry of various sorts, seal stones, cups and vases, and daggers. Some of these items appear to have been made expressly for use as burial gifts since they show no signs of use. Indeed, some of the jewelry and tools are of such delicate construction that they would not survive ordinary use.

In addition to the burial gifts that were interred along with the bodies (these were communal tombs containing multiple burials) archaeologists have found cups, jugs and libation pitchers in the anterooms and in the open plazas around the buildings. These utensils point to religious activities of some sort that took place in or near the tombs: an ancestor cult or cult of the dead. Many of the bodies were also given secondary burial; that is, some time after the funeral the corpse was removed from the original funeral display, dismembered and interred elsewhere in the tomb, often en masse with other bodies.

We may speculate on the nature of these earliest religious activities using the physical form of the ritual items as our guide. Many of the pitchers used for libations are a female shape, with the liquid pouring out through holes in the breasts. Other rhyta (libation pitchers) have been found in the form of cattle. Although these are often referred to as 'bull-vessels,' they might just as well be cows since there is no indication one way or the other to designate their sex. We modern folk tend to forget that until the late 19th century all cattle, both male and female, had horns. These animal pitchers have holes in the mouth for the pouring of wine. So here we have the oft-repeated image of mother's milk and animals as sustenance. And remember, these utensils were used to make offerings to or about the dead, who

Pottery libation pitcher from Mochlos

are given gifts of food and drink worldwide to sustain them in the afterlife.

There is also an interesting class of small cups often called 'sheep-bells' due to their conical, bell-like shape. These vessels have two protrusions on the base with a sort of handle in between so they would not stand up if set on a table or other solid surface. When they are placed with the mouth down (upside-down, if you think of them as cups), the two protrusions on the base look like upraised arms, with the handle as the head. The conical shape of the cup implies a long gown on the figure. Now, most of these cups had holes in the ends of the protrusions so that when the cup was turned upright and filled with liquid it looked remarkably like an udder spilling forth milk. This double image is a form of magic, one item becoming two different things depending on how it is positioned. It also reinforces the animal (goat, sheep or cow) and mother's milk symbolism.

Though the tombs were made according to many different designs, they have one important feature in common: they contained multiple burials. Thus they were a focal point for bringing together families and communities. The families of the dead gathered at these tombs to enact rituals and to offer wine, food and gifts to the spirits of their ancestors. So even in the earliest days of Minoan society, a religious center served as a gathering place for the local people. In fact, there is some speculation that even as early as the late third millennium BCE there were priests and/or priestesses whose sole function was to tend these many tombs and perform the appropriate rituals. If this is the case, these people were the precursors of the clergy who inhabited the great temples many centuries later.

Let us contemplate the specific rituals the Minoans may have performed. Obviously, there is a limited amount of time after a death in which the family can perform the funeral. Therefore no particular season or calendar date can be put on primary burials, since people have an uncanny knack for dying without any regard for the convenience of their families and friends. However, throughout the third millennium BCE and to some extent into the second millennium, the Minoans carried on a practice called secondary burial. This means exactly what it sounds like. Long after the individual's funeral, perhaps a number of years later, the family would remove the now-clean skeleton from its first resting place, dismember it and reinter it, either in a different area or room of the tomb or in a large *pithos* (storage jar).

This practice may sound odd to us but it was quite common in ancient times and is still practiced in some rural areas around the Mediterranean even today. You see, a number of cultures recognized two stages of death and dealt with each one separately. While the corpse was still intact enough to look even vaguely like the living person to whom it had belonged, the dead person's spirit was thought to linger nearby, to be in a state of waiting. What the spirit was waiting for was the complete dissolution of its former body. Only when the body had decomposed to nothing but bones did the spirit's connection with it cease. Only then could the spirit move on to the next realm, to the afterlife proper.

It seems likely that there was a special ritual associated with this secondary burial. Since the Minoan tombs contained multiple burials it is likely there would have been a need or desire for this sort of ritual on a regular basis. Judging by the large number of cups, bowls, jugs and animal bones found at these sites, we can conjecture a feast-type gathering in celebration of the passing over of the ancestors into the next realm. In ancient Crete, with its lack of supermarkets and hothouse gardens, such a ritual could only have been held at one time of the year: harvest.

We can begin to piece together the first harvest-time ritual the Minoans likely celebrated, a ceremony to honor their ancestors, those who had died and moved on to the afterlife. In these rituals they ate abundant, nourishing food and poured libations from vessels that depicted the life-sustaining qualities of that most sacred substance, mother's milk. This mystical balance shows the Minoans' early reverence for the feminine and their sanctification of the grand cycle of death and life.

This symbology also underscores a theme common to rituals centering around the dead – the vigorous continuation of life among those still living. In addition to the eating and drinking, there may have been other activities that emphasized the strength and youth of the ritual attendees. Among the finds at Koumasa on the south coast of Crete was a libation pitcher shaped like a bull or cow. This piece has two human figures hanging onto the horns of the animal, an early foreshadowing of the famed Minoan bull-leaping competitions. Such a feat of strength and courage would serve to emphasize the vitality of those still alive, thus providing a counterpoint to the focus on those who had died.

This collection of evidence for the ancestor or 'cult of the dead' ritual also gives us a glimpse of a deeper spirituality on early Crete. The many female-shaped vessels and figurines can be seen as a representation of the divine, life-giving feminine principle. In other words, a goddess. These artifacts may be the earliest face of the Great Goddess of life and death whom the Minoans came to call Ariadne.

Building Up to Gather Together

When most people think about ancient Crete, the image of the magnificent temples springs to mind. We must remember, of course, that the Minoans had a highly developed culture and religion for nearly a thousand years before they built the first temples. But the temples make a stronger impression on the modern psyche than any other relic from their civilization. These buildings were the crowning glory of four of Crete's urban centers – Knossos, Phaistos, Malia and Zakros. And ever since Sir Arthur Evans unearthed the first one at the turn of the 20th century, people have erringly called them *palaces*.

When Evans excavated Knossos and examined his finds, he was working from the viewpoint of a wealthy, imperialistic, chauvinistic Englishman. Like the remainder of the archaeological community at the time, he knew next to nothing about real life on ancient Crete. So when he found the remains of vast, many-roomed buildings, lavishly decorated and intricately designed, he assumed they were the palaces of Crete's princes and kings. In fact, he even put specific monarchic titles on different rooms as he found them. When he came to one of the largest rooms at Knossos, extravagantly painted with wall-to-wall, floor-to-ceiling frescoes and containing a large, built-in high-backed chair, he called it the King's Throne Room. The only problem is, there was never a king on Crete. In fact, the 'Throne Room' appears to be a ritual setting for a high priestess and her entourage.

We now know that the towns all across the island based their social structure on trade and religion, being ruled by a number of wealthy merchant families and a priestly class. This 'government-less' arrangement was widely admired throughout the ancient world, though perhaps not so much for its lack of bureaucracy as for its incredible wealth and peace. The later Spartans, who also lived without a central government or monarchy, are said to have based their constitution on the structure of Minoan society.

After all this time we have finally come to realize that Crete had no monarchy. But that leaves us with one problem: if there was no monarchy, then who used these buildings that looked so much like palaces to a wealthy Englishman? Of course, the obvious solution is that they were not palaces at all, but temples, centers for the ancient and often extravagant Minoan rituals and ceremonies. These striking buildings, the centerpieces of the cities they served, were designed specifically for the role they played in Minoan society. We can even deduce some of the specifics of religious practice from the temple structures themselves.

First, let us look at the external appearance of the temples. They were situated in the center of the towns, often on the highest point of the land. Large mansions (often referred to as villas) belonging to the wealthiest merchants were built very close by, often right up against the palace perimeter. The temples were all unfortified; the walls that enclosed them were designed simply to delineate the edge of the property and were for the most part indefensible. There were large open plazas in front of the buildings where the people could gather for various occasions. Thus these buildings do not look like what we think of as palaces. They stood as central meeting places for the religious and economic life of the cities, just as temples did in many other ancient cultures around the world.

Every other advanced Bronze Age culture had large sacred buildings of one sort or another. We find temples and sacred structures in Egypt, Greece, Palestine, Syria – throughout the ancient world. In fact, the palatial buildings on Crete mirror in many ways the temples found throughout the Near East. Of course, the Minoans had long-term contact with societies from Spain to Asia Minor, trading ideas along with consumer goods. The temples on Crete and the towns that grew up around them reflect not only the Minoans' particular religious practices but also the spiritual philosophy of much of the Bronze Age world.

These grand buildings that we have so long called palaces are each the focal point of a Minoan town. In the ancient world the design and layout of towns as well as buildings was considered to have a sacred aspect, a physical reflection of the celestial and spiritual order. In this world view the central structure or focal point of a town was considered sacred, a roughly mirrored physical image of the divine center of the universe from which all things emanate. In some societies this *omphalos*, or divine center, was a plaza. In some societies it was a temple. So it was with Crete.

When we look at the layout of these four expansive buildings

27

in four separate towns (Knossos, Phaistos, Malia and Zakros) we discover that they all have similar structures and floor plans. In the ancient world, where social fashion rarely extended to architecture, this similarity must be attributed to ideology. In other words, the buildings are so very alike because they all served a similar function in the spiritual lives of the Minoans. Their functions were so similar from town to town that, except for Zakros, the central plazas of the palaces have nearly identical dimensions despite the fact that the palaces as a whole vary greatly in size.

Like many sacred structures in the ancient world, the temples on Crete are situated within meaningful, symbolic landscape features. 'Horned' double-peak mountains, symbolic of the goddess' breasts and the horns of the life-giving cattle, have a prominent place near all the temples, as well as being represented in the carving and decoration on the temples themselves. The view along the roads that approach the temples highlights these mountain peaks and other symbolic parts of the surrounding land that become visible one by one as a traveler nears the building.

All four palaces are also carefully oriented to the four compass points even though they are situated on very different terrain. This precise orientation is indicative worldwide of sacred buildings. Besides reinforcing the view of the palaces as temples, this gives us a very important piece of information about the Minoans' spirituality. It tells us that they honored the four cardinal directions and incorporated them into their religious practices.

Of the four directions, the west seems to have been especially associated with the sacred. The central courts in all four temples are lined along the west facade with a row of small shrines. The temples' west wings are also replete with shrines and at Zakros the west wing was found full of a variety of ritual implements. It is along the west wing of these structures that the open plaza, or public court, is located. The western sides of the temples open onto this public setting where people gathered for rituals.

It is interesting to note that the sacred west wing is also the site, in all four temples, of the earliest grain storage rooms. There are also the remains of processional pathways across the plazas, pathways that pass alongside these granaries. This setup suggests a ritual procession during a festival in which the grain was an important aspect, perhaps a harvest festival. Though these western granaries were eventually abandoned in favor of grain storage in large jars within the temple itself, the plazas continued to be used for ritual gatherings. These public courts at all the temples were eventually augmented with large stone platforms. Presumably, on these platforms stood those of the priestly class who officiated the various ceremonies and perhaps prominent townsfolk as well.

At any rate, public ritual was an important aspect of Minoan life. We can see these gatherings as a continuation of the practice begun centuries earlier in the courtyards around the first tombs. Communal religious practice was a basic part of the spiritual life of the ancient Minoans throughout the lifespan of their culture.

It is interesting to note that in one striking way the Minoan temples differ radically from other Bronze Age structures of similar purpose. Many cultures throughout the world built temples about the same time the Minoans did, but most of the other temples have one common feature: they were built as monuments to powerful rulers and leaders. These temples often commemorate battles and conquests, glorifying one person above all others and even highlighting the taking of prisoners and the execution of the conquered peoples. There are no such depictions anywhere in the Minoan temples. In fact, the only representation of a leader at all is that of a priestess (or goddess) receiving ceremonial tribute on a fresco in the temple at Knossos.

The Minoans built their temples with a different purpose – not to separate the people from the exalted leaders but to bring the people into the expression of the divine and make them feel a part of it. Rather than monumental friezes and giant statues that dwarf the people and make them feel inferior, the temples on Crete contain small shrines, beautiful artwork and accessible ritual areas. These features would have drawn ritual participants into the scene rather than separating them from it. This attitude of inclusion and the emphasis on the divine within everyone was unusual in the Bronze Age world and is rare even today. This closeness and inclusion brings spirituality to a personal level and aids in healing the rift between the individual and the divine.

Another way to connect with the religious practices of the ancient Minoans is through their art. Their greatest contribution to the world of art is their numerous frescoes, some covering entire walls and hallways. One of the most expansive frescoes yet

Young men bearing offerings, Corridor of the Processions, Knossos Temple

found is located in the entrance hallway of the temple at Knossos. This long corridor is decorated on both sides with depictions of men and women in some sort of ritual procession, hence the title Corridor of the Processions. The people in the frescoes are carrying various items – jugs, pitchers, garments – toward a central female figure. This priestess is accepting the people's tribute, for she is the earthly face of the goddess.

The earthly face of the goddess: this concept is central to the Minoans' religious practice. The 'snake-goddess' figurines that typify the modern world's view of ancient Crete are not goddesses at all. They are priestesses. The Minoans rarely depicted actual deities in their art, for they apparently believed that we cannot know or understand what the gods and goddesses really look like. They believed, instead, that a priestess could take on the aspect of the goddess she served, become possessed as it were, and *become* the goddess for the time of the ritual.

This attitude differs radically from our modern concept of our separation from the divine. The Minoans knew their deities as living, breathing participants in the glory of ritual. The officiant did not stand in the ritual area and call to the deity as many religious leaders do worldwide in various ceremonies. Instead, the participants gathered in the ritual area as the priestess prepared herself unseen in an adjacent room. When the priestess entered the ritual area to perform a ceremony, she was no longer a priestess; she was the goddess incarnate. The garments she wore during the ritual might even be displayed afterward as sacred objects, having touched the body of the living goddess. Just as the design of Minoan shrines and temples drew the people into their religion rather than separating them from it, so their religious practice brought them face-to-face with their gods.

Following the Sacred Path

The temples, shrines and mansions in ancient Crete were full of people. Of course, many of the temple inhabitants were artists and craftsmen, administrators and servants (and possibly slaves – Crete was not a utopia by any means). But a sizable portion of the temple population, and the population of the island as a whole, were priestesses and priests. These people gave their lives over to their religion and held no other jobs. They performed public and private rituals both at the temples and at shrines in the towns and out in the countryside, and administered the goods and services that flowed in and out of the temple complexes. For their dedication, the temples housed, fed and supported them.

As we look at depictions of priestesses and priests in Minoan frescoes, pottery and other sources, we must keep in mind the context within which these representations were created. In the Minoan religious framework priestesses and priests embodied the goddesses and gods of their world. When a member of the priestly class donned his or her ritual garments and performed a ceremony, that person became a deity incarnate. We rarely find depictions of goddesses and gods on Crete simply because the Minoans did not think of their deities as separate from the priestesses and priests who served them. Thus, in Minoan art we find depictions of human beings performing rituals of various sorts. But we also find figures which appear to be members of the priestly class in settings in which we might otherwise expect to see a deity. For the Minoans, these *were* depictions of their deities, for they saw their goddesses and gods in the people who served them.

A few physical characteristics typify the priestly class and separate them from the remainder of the Minoan people. To begin with, the priestesses and priests dressed distinctly.

The women wore headgear that symbolized their devotion to the goddess. We find depictions of priestesses with headbands, hats and coronets as a symbol of their office. Headdresses adorned with lilies are a particular attribute of priestesses and also of the Minoan version of that female mythological creature, the sphinx.

The priestess' garments were similar to those worn by most well-to-do Minoan women – flounced skirts, tight girdles and simple tops – but priestesses also wore aprons bearing emblems of their patron deities. Their garments were often decorated with animals and plants symbolic of the faces of the goddess – griffins, crocuses and so forth. The tight-fitting girdles and wide-open bodices of their outfits served to emphasize two aspects of the feminine: the priestesses' (and thus the goddess') sexuality as well as the maternal comfort of the breast. Though this symbolism was surely apparent in ordinary women's clothing, it was purposely underscored through ritual as the priestesses embodied the various aspects of the goddess.

The priestesses' garments played a special role in the religious life of the Minoans. Before performing a ritual, the priestess was ceremonially dressed and decorated in order to fulfill her role as the goddess incarnate. The garments she wore for the ritual, especially the skirt and girdle, then became sacred, as if the goddess herself had worn them. They were sometimes hung on special stands or columns for display and further worship. We might find this 'wardrobe worship' a bit odd, but the Minoans considered the priestess' ceremonial clothing to be hallowed objects, just as modern pagans might consider their ritual robes and other gear sacred. We also see such a belief in the Catholic practice of relic worship, in which people revere a garment or personal item that belonged to a saint. We see in these practices the concept of a physical item becoming holy or sacred when it comes in contact with the divine.

The Minoan priests had their own special form of dress as well, though their garments were not given further reverence after the ritual was over, as far as we know. Young men in training for the priesthood often participated in ceremonies in which they impersonated the young, virile aspect of the god. For these rituals the young men wore short, tight-fitting kilts with pronounced phallus sheaths reminiscent of medieval European codpieces. They went bare-chested, often carrying a spear or other weapon. This clothing emphasized the virility, strength and youth of these young men and thus of their god.

The older priests also wore distinctive clothing: long robes with diagonal trim and tassels, a style reserved only for them. They are often depicted with short hair, bangs and beards in contrast to the long hair and clean-shaven faces of the fashionable Minoan men. This style separated the mature priests both from the general populace and from the younger men of the priestly class.

The male and female clergy of ancient Crete wore easily recognizable garments that distinguished them from each other and from the other classes of the island populace. But during the later Minoan empire the members of the priestly class also shared a garment in common. Both sexes wore ankle-length animal-hide skirts for certain rituals that appear to have centered around animal sacrifice, usually of goats or sheep. The sacrifice itself was the task of the priest, while the priestess had the responsibility of libations and the presentation of other offerings. The dress of the clergy in this situation reflected their close link with the animal they sacrificed to their deities, perhaps as a way of sharing food with them. The early Minoans did not practice animal sacrifice as part of their religious devotion. It is possible that they picked up this tradition from the Mycenaeans, who began to migrate onto the island toward the end of the empire.

In addition to distinctive clothing, the priestly class had a set of symbolic objects which denoted their sanctity and power. Priestesses and priests are depicted with these objects in frescoes, on seal-stones, and in numerous other artistic settings. These symbols of deities and religious authority also decorate shrines and ritual sites. The clergy wore these images on their ritual garments and wielded the actual objects in ceremonies, processions and audiences.

Priests are most often depicted with small curved axes of a design generally considered to have come from Syria. It is interesting to note that the unique robes the priests wore are probably also a Syrian design, especially since the first settlers came to Crete from Asia Minor. Minoan priests are also shown holding stone maces, bows and lances. All of these items are implements of hunting and sacrifice, two roles the priests fulfilled in ritual and ceremony.

Priestess pouring a libation, Hagia Triada sarcophagus

Priestesses had their own symbols for use during ritual. They are occasionally depicted wearing crowns of horns, linking them to the old lunar cow-goddess and to the later bull who represented so many aspects of the Minoan god. Priestesses also carried the crook, an instrument for herding sheep and goats, and the famed labrys or double axe. The labrys was not used as a sacrificial axe, though many modern fictional accounts suggest otherwise. The labrys was basically a stylized butterfly, one of the symbols of the goddess who changes with the seasons and stages of life, an emblem of her regenerative and transformative power. This sacred tool also reflects the seasonal vegetative and agricultural cycle the Minoans associated with their deities, for it is shaped like the hoe axes the island inhabitants used to clear land for planting. It also looks very much like a woman's vulva, making it a powerful symbol of the feminine, both human and divine. It was solely a symbolic object, but a powerful one, representing the cycles of life, death and rebirth.

Divine Shrines

Let us look now at the settings in which the Minoans practiced their religion, especially during the later years of their culture. The most common and easily identifiable place of worship on Crete is the shrine. Several different types of shrines, with different purposes and dedicated to different deities, are found in abundance throughout the temples and many of the villas. Some simple shrines have also been found in smaller houses belonging to Crete's 'middle class.' Ritual and religious observance was an important part of life in ancient Crete among the lay people as well as the clergy.

One type of ritual setting which archaeologists and, indeed, most modern people, find odd is the sort of shrine known as the lustral basin. This consists of a room with a large sunken section that gives the impression of a basin or built-in bathtub. The sunken section has steps leading down into it from the regular floor level. Although some archaeologists have suggested that these sunken chambers were ritual bathing areas, or even ordinary bathrooms, it is now believed that they were a particular type of ritual space that did not involve bathing.

These odd rooms were used for rituals in which only a few people participated, since the sunken areas are quite small. In some cases there are balconies on the upper story above the ritual room from which select people could observe the ritual below. It is possible that these sunken areas were used for initiatory rituals, especially since a number of them have special anterooms through which the participants must enter. Since these areas are sunken, they may have symbolized a journey from the temple into the underworld. At any rate, they are an unusual addition to our store of knowledge about religion in ancient Crete.

Another misnamed Minoan shrine type is the pillar crypt. To the modern ear the word 'crypt' suggests a dank, creepy, almost dungeon-like room. This is not the case at all. It is true that these shrines are located in basement rooms with little light available from windows or skylights. But they were dry, well-kept rooms, painted and decorated with religious symbols and figures. The pillars that give this type of shrine its name are just that – columns used to support the weight of the upper floors. But in these shrines the pillars were also focal points for rituals and libations.

These shrines were probably used for ceremonies associated with ancestor rituals or cult of the dead practices. Some of the earlier pillar crypts were built adjacent to tombs and the later ones in the temples certainly evoke the feeling of a tomb. The pillar crypts that were built into the temples at Knossos and Malia, and in several of the large villas, are also connected to the grain storage rooms. Some scholars have suggested that this connection, along with the apparent funereal cult use, indicates a mythos involving a grain-deity in a ritual cycle of birth, death and rebirth. This cycle would be similar to that of the western European gods of the fields and to the classical Greek tales of Demeter and Persephone.

The pillar crypts were decorated with ritual symbols, mostly double axes and occasionally sacred horns, on the walls and especially on the pillars. Some of the pillars have small ledges on which ritual tools or offerings could be placed. The double axe symbols on the walls are echoed by special axe-stands next to the pillars, in which a labrys would have been placed during ceremonies. An interesting feature of these shrines is that many of the pillars were set in the center of depressions in the floor. Small rectangular hollows separate from the pillars have also been found in some of the shrines. These sunken areas, odd to the modern eye, would have been used for the pouring of libations during ceremonies so that the wine or other liquid did not spill all over the floor. Since the receptacles are sunk into the floor we can also postulate that the libations were directed to the underworld, the abode of the dead and their guardian deities.

Another type of shrine, common in Crete all the way from the third millennium BCE until the end of the empire, was the dining shrine. A sacred dining room might seem odd to us in the modern world, when many of us do not even sit down to family dinners on a regular basis any more. But in the ancient world, inviting a deity to dine with you was the most basic form of worship and communion.

On Crete the sacred dining areas were usually part of a complex of rooms. These auxiliary rooms included food preparation areas such as small mills for grinding grain to be made into bread and small hearths for cooking meat, either regular food or animal sacrifices. There were also storage rooms for food and the many dishes, cups and bowls that were kept apart for this sacred use. The dining areas themselves often included built-in benches around the walls. These were used to seat the participants and to hold food and serving ware until it was needed. Everything involved in the sacred meals, from food to dishes, was kept in its own special place and used only for dining rituals, the Minoans' communion with their gods.

Into the Lap of the Mother

A common feature of Minoan spiritual life, and one often overlooked in favor of the impressive temples, is the shrines and religious sanctuaries on the open land, in caves and up in the mountains. These nature sanctuaries and shrines were the gathering places for the common folk, those who were not of high enough social standing to attend the temple rituals and those who lived too far out in the country to reach the towns with any regularity. These sacred places in nature were an integral part of regular worship long after the temples and urban shrines were abandoned.

Among the most awe-inspiring of the Minoan nature sanctuaries are the shrines and sacred places located at the peaks of the sharp and craggy central mountain range. While some of these sanctuaries were simply flat, open mountaintop spaces where the local shepherds and farmers deposited sacred offerings, a few of the mountaintop sanctuaries were built up formally. They might have a table or small altar on which to place figurines, lamps and other offerings. The larger mountaintop sanctuaries had buildings which served as temples; the sanctuary on the mountain of Juktas near Knossos even had a wall built around it.

Regardless of the degree to which these sanctuaries were built up and decorated, they were a nexus for ritual visitation by everyone from the poorest shepherds to delegates from the temples. Minoans continued to worship at these sacred places for decades and, in some instances, centuries after the temples had ceased to perform a ceremonial function.

The people who visited these shrines would have traveled up the steep mountains to seek the aid of the deities who resided there or to offer them thanks. Small figurines abound at these sites – clay and bronze animals of all sorts, men and women, even disembodied limbs, perhaps left by people requesting specific types of healing. These figurines would have been offered at the mountaintop shrines to ask for help from the resident goddess or god. Small personal tokens and mementos such as bracelets, amulets, seal-stones and swords were left in thanks to the deities for their aid and protection.

In addition to individual pilgrimages, these mountaintop sanctuaries were also the sites of regular festivals and public ceremonies. One prominent feature of these festivals was bonfires, attested by thick deposits of ash at the larger sanctuaries. The figurines and other offerings that the people brought to the sanctuaries and placed on the altars throughout the year would have been thrown into the fire at the large festivals, finalizing the ritual for which they were intended.

We do not know which deities, either goddesses or gods or both, were worshipped at all the mountaintop sanctuaries. It is likely that each sanctuary had its own local deity and sacred festival, much as is the case today throughout Greece. We do know that the god Zagreus was connected with Mt. Dikte in central Crete, as was his mother Amalthea. The tale of Zagreus' birth from the Great Mother Goddess is an important part of the Minoan mythological cycle. Perhaps other mountains were known as the birthplaces of other deities. At any rate, the local people found these stunning, often snow-capped peaks to be appropriate abodes for their goddesses and gods.

Equally awe-inspiring but physically antithetical to the mountaintop sanctuaries are the shrines the Minoans created within the many caves on their island. In the mythological tale of Zagreus' birth on Mt. Dikte, his mother Rhea placed him in a cave to keep him safe as a small infant. Caves, like mountains, figure prominently in the Minoan religious archetype. A number of the cave sanctuaries on Crete were the sites of large gatherings, much as the mountaintop sanctuaries were used for public ceremonies.

Since the caves have their own walls and roofs, the people who visited them simply provided altars and small tables on which to place offerings.

In these cave shrines excavators have found votive figurines similar to those from the mountaintop shrines – animal and human forms, small tools or weapons, and personal mementos. Evidence of feasting has also been found in the form of heaps of grain and grain storage jars, small hearths and animal bones, and plentiful pottery cups, bowls and pitchers. But, unlike the festivals held on the mountaintops, there were no bonfires in the caves. Instead, when the participants chose to dispose of their offerings to the deities, they threw them down clefts in the rocks or into the subterranean pools of water that collected in the caves.

Among the cave shrines found throughout the island are smaller ones apparently used only by the few people who lived right around them. There is no evidence of large festivals or other gatherings in these shrines. The locals who visited them brought votive offerings and set up altars, just as in the larger cave sanctuaries. It is possible that many of the farmers and shepherds who lived far out in the country had no nearby alternative for their rites and ceremonies. These small cave shrines as well as the larger ones continued in use for a number of centuries after the Minoans had ceased to visit the temples for religious events.

It is likely that the caves, like the mountaintops, were each sacred to their own local deity. One cave shrine whose goddess we can name is the cave of Amnissos near Knossos. This particular sanctuary was sacred to the goddess Eleithyia, the divine midwife and goddess of birth. The connection of caves with birth is also echoed in the myth of the god Zagreus.

Birth as a psychological process can also involve initiations of various sorts, including rites of passage for coming of age or joining a group. While there is no direct evidence to link all cave sanctuaries with birth imagery and deities, caves figure so prominently throughout human cultures as womb symbols that it is difficult to ignore this connection. Regardless, cave sanctuaries abounded on Crete and were an integral part of the religious life of rural and urban Minoans for many centuries.

Chapter 4

The House of the Double Axe

Ariadne's Thread

When we think of Crete, among the many images that come to mind is the famed labyrinth, the maze Theseus encountered in his heroic adventure to defeat the Minotaur. But this superficial depiction of the tale of the goddess Ariadne and her initiate reveals only the surface of a centuries-old mythological cycle that tells us much about the spirituality and psyche of the ancient Minoans.

The labyrinth is a component of the mythology of many ancient cultures, Crete among them. The well-known legend of Theseus and his voyage to Crete actually dates to the Mycenaean period, long after the civilization recognizable as Minoan had ceased to exist. This legend was built on the basis of the beliefs and practices of the Minoans as they were handed down for many generations before the encroachment of the mainland Greeks. One major facet of these beliefs is the role of the goddess in personal initiation and enlightenment. It is in this role that Ariadne heals, and it is this function that inspired the concept of the labyrinth.

The Minoan goddess who held the fate of mortals in her hand was Ariadne, the spinner of the thread of fate and weaver of the web of life. While later Mycenaean legends reduced her to a simple Minoan maiden whose job was weaving and spinning, her earlier guise was far more powerful. The thread she spun was that of each individual's path in life, their destiny if they chose to follow it. And the legend of Theseus' adventure in the labyrinth follows Ariadne's thread.

When one culture overtakes another, the conquering culture often reduces the deities of the conquered culture to demigods or mere legendary figures. This was the case when the Mycenaeans overtook the Minoans and imposed the mainland Greek pantheon on the island's culture. One of the casualties of this cultural shift was the powerful story of the goddess Ariadne and her sacred labyrinth of initiation. With the coming of the Mycenaeans, it was reduced to the legend of a mere maiden and the boy she aided. But we can reconstruct the original sacred tale from the later story.

The legend of Theseus begins with his sea voyage to Crete from mainland Greece. His goal was to rescue the Greek youths who had been abducted to Crete as tribute to the Minoan king. Never mind that the Minoans never had a king; the Mycenaeans did and they are the ones who concocted this part of the story. Theseus made his way to Crete by volunteering to be one of those sent to the island as tribute.

The legend continues with Theseus sneaking into the palace at Knossos and befriending the maiden or servant Ariadne, though in some tales she is called the daughter of the Minos-King. Of course, the legend fails to mention that the palace was in reality a temple and that Ariadne was one of the names of Crete's Great Goddess. In order to defeat the imaginary Minoan king and free the Greek youths, Theseus had to find his way through the maze of the labyrinth and slay the Minotauros, a ferocious creature who was half man and half bull. Theseus succeeded in his task with Ariadne's help. She furnished him with a ball of string that marked his path into the labyrinth and thus allowed him to find his way out.

An interesting postscript to the story involves Theseus' relationship with Ariadne. He had promised to marry her, either because he fell in love with her or in exchange for her help in the labyrinth, depending on which version of the tale you encounter. The two sailed toward Greece but stopped at the island of Dia, where they disembarked. After a short stay on the island, Theseus and his crew sailed away, leaving Ariadne all alone.

Some accounts suggest that Theseus left her for another woman and others tell of Dionysus' desire for Ariadne and his threats to Theseus if he did not leave her.

The end of the tale has Dionysus appearing to Ariadne as she sits crying on the deserted shore. He comforts her and marries her, presenting her with Thetis' crown as a token of his devotion. This crown was crafted by the divine smith Hephaestos of gold set with red gems in the shape of roses. Legend states that Dionysus later set this crown out among the stars, where it became the Corona Borealis (Crown of Lights) to remind everyone of his love for Ariadne.

Thus goes the Greek legend. But let us look at the underlying mythology that is purely Minoan, before the later influence of the mainland Greeks. First, we know that Ariadne was a face of the goddess for the Minoans. Her functions involved helping her followers find their path in life and aiding them through initiation and healing. These functions inspired the symbology of the spinner with her spindle, drawing out the thread of each person's life path, a symbolism which degraded into a vision of a maiden spinning for her masters (the Greek gods) in Mycenaean times. One of Ariadne's tools for leading individuals through initiations was the labyrinth.

The legend of Theseus has colored modern thinking about what the labyrinth might have been. There is no archaeological evidence of an actual labyrinth at Knossos or any of the other Minoan towns. However, there are labyrinth-type patterns in mosaic tiles in a number of locations on Crete, Thera and mainland Greece. The main characteristic of these patterns is that they are not mazes in the modern sense. A maze is a puzzle in which one can make wrong turns and get lost. In other words, there is no obvious direct path but rather a number of possible routes, only one of which actually leads to the center of the maze. This is not the case in a labyrinth.

A labyrinth contains only one possible route to the center and thus only one way out. It looks like a squared-off spiral, its path curving around itself outward from the center. It is not possible to become lost in this sort of arrangement. The point is not to puzzle out the correct path to the center; there is only one way. The labyrinth must have held some other function.

Indeed, the labyrinth and its powerful imagery are a crucial part of Ariadne's bag of tricks. The name itself belies its use: *labyrinth* means *house of the labrys*, or double axe. This ceremonial tool, long believed by modern archaeologists to be a sacrificial weapon, was in reality a powerful symbol that was never used as an axe. The labrys is a stylized butterfly, the symbol of transformation and regeneration. What a powerful and appropriate symbol for the rebirth of initiation that took place in the labyrinth. The blade of the labrys also resembles a woman's vulva, the doorway through which we are born into this world.

The spiraling path of the labyrinth was a part of the initiation ceremonies used by Ariadne's devotees. The individual facing initiation would be facing his or her deepest fears, those things that keep us from advancing on our life paths. Then as now, initiation involved a losing of self, a symbolic death followed by spiritual rebirth. The individual being initiated would move symbolically through the labyrinth, away from the outer world and toward the inner world of self-knowledge and truth, toward the center of the labyrinth. Ariadne's thread, the knowledge that a spark of the divine lies at the core of every being, kept the individual linked to the gods even when separated from mankind. And at the center lay the darkest fears, the monster of the psyche – the Minotaur.

Though we most often associate the labyrinth with the bull-monster Minotaur, let us look first at another animal whose symbology is tied to this tale. The animal sacred to Theseus is the crane, a graceful bird that bred along the shores of Crete in ancient times. The crane also gave its name to a ritual, the Crane Dance. This ritual dance drew the participants in a spiral around a horned altar, mimicking Theseus' journey into the center of the labyrinth and out again. But the dance is a double-layered symbol. On the surface it symbolizes the mythological tale of a boy's adventure on Crete. On a deeper level, though, it symbolizes the initiatory journey each person must make toward the center of their being and back again. This journey has at its center the other animal involved in this tale, the bull.

The Moon-Bull, the Minotaur found at the center of the labyrinth, was originally an animal consort to the Minoan goddess. Toward the end of the Minoan empire the Minotaur took on greater power and a cult grew around his worship, a monotheistic cult reminiscent of the later Mithraic traditions around the Mediterranean. But his earlier form was that of the goddess' underworld consort. Ariadne was often seen as the bright goddess whose consort, like the later Greek Hades, ruled the underworld.

Our Judeo-Christian view of Hell as the underworld often clouds our interpretation of such roles. In ancient times, however, the underworld was just as important (and positive) an aspect of the cycle of life, death and rebirth as the upper world. And to the goddess' consort fell the crucial task of overseeing the dark half of the cycle, the underworld journey from death to life again. The consort took a number of forms, all of which metamorphosed in the later Greek pantheon. The Serpent Consort became Hermes, the Stag Consort became the Horned One, and the Bull Consort became the Minotaur.

Perhaps in Ariadne's initiation rites the purpose of facing the dark side of the divine was not, after all, to conquer it. It is far more likely that the postulant who reached the center of the labyrinth had the goal of accepting the Minotaur into its rightful place in the human psyche, just as it had an accepted place in Minoan mythology. Even in cultures such as ancient Crete which hold both sides of the cycle in equal regard, the portion of the cycle symbolized by the underworld can be daunting, even frightening. Those things in the universe which are the hardest to understand and accept – death, fear, darkness, loss – are a necessary part of the balance above and below. Ariadne's task is to bring all these qualities to the attention of her followers, that they may accept them as part of the great cycle. This is one form of healing that Ariadne brings to us.

Descendants of the Sacred Maze

One derivation of the Labyrinth tradition that made its way into Europe is the letter labyrinth, a sacred patterned word puzzle that holds a mystery within its letter combinations. These puzzles date at least as far back as Imperial Rome and were common throughout Europe until the early 18th century CE. In (pre-medieval) pagan times these letter labyrinths were used in magical workings, much as modern pagans might write a spell chant or draw a diagram. As Christianity gained sway these puzzles continued in use, though for meditative and prayerful purposes or as protections on churches and other religious sites.

These magical puzzles involved a phrase or set of words written to form a specific shape such as a square, circle, or cross. The arrangement of letters allows the user to discern not only the original words but also new words and phrases, imparting some insight due to the unexpected meanings. The most common example of these letter labyrinths is a simple Latin one in the shape of a square:

```
S A T O R
A R E P O
T E N E T
O P E R A
R O T A S
```

This letter puzzle dates to ancient Roman times and was apparently a popular charm in common use, having been found at a number of archaeological sites. It roughly translates as, 'The sower Sator holds the wheels as his work.' This may refer to the agricultural cycles and the wheel of the year as celebrated by the pagan Romans. The name Sator is possibly that of a regional grain god or demigod.

The Sator Square is a simple example of a form that can be extraordinarily complex. There are examples of letter labyrinths from medieval churches in which the letters form crosses or labyrinth-type mazes. One- or two-word phrases can fill out large forms or whole sentences can be rearranged to show different meanings. The transposition of one thing into another is, after all, an act of magic.

Thus we see the transformative qualities of the Minoan labyrinth even in something as simple as a word puzzle. The relative simplicity of these letter labyrinths together with their multi-layered meanings and magical connotations make them an attractive addition to the neo-pagan repertoire. They can be constructed in any language, with the energy, creativity and purpose of the maker to guide their shape. In fact, the crossword puzzle you find in your daily newspaper is a direct descendant of these magical word-puzzles. It's something to think about over your morning coffee.

Chapter 5

Ariadne's Tribe:
The Minoan Pantheon

The Family Tree

In many of the European pantheons we encounter a 'family tree' of deities crowned by a great father-god such as Odin in the Norse pantheon, or a divine couple such as Zeus and Hera from classical Greece. The Minoan pantheon, however, was arranged differently from the other European systems. Over the spiritual lives of the Minoans presided a Great Mother Goddess, the creator of all things, who ruled without a consort. Through the ages the name the Minoans originally gave her has faded away, but we still know what the Greeks called one of her aspects: Ariadne.

Many goddesses of Ariadne's tribe followed her example and took their place in the pantheon without a male consort. Only toward the end of Minoan civilization, when the mainland Greeks (Mycenaeans) exerted their social and religious influence on the people of Crete, did male consorts become a requirement. Of course, there were plenty of gods for the Minoans to revere and work with, but they stood on their own, as did the goddesses. Apparently the Minoans prized individuality, a value we hold dear in our own society today.

It is easy to see how such a goddess-crowned pantheon could have developed. The Minoans themselves were an egalitarian society. Their deities mirrored the way the people lived. The primordial goddesses of earth and sea were just that; they had no 'other half.' Rhea (as the Greeks called her) had no consort; she was simply Earth or Creation. She was indeed the primordial Great Goddess of Bronze Age Crete and the Aegean islands. In fact, all the way up until the time of the Hellenic invasions she was seen as the Universal Mother without a consort, even though other goddesses developed partners at an earlier date. In her goat-form Aega, Rhea was the founder of Aegean civilization, whose people named themselves after her. As for the sea, the Greek god Poseidon was created by the Greeks from the Minoan goddess Posidaeja. The Minoans did not recognize any masculine symbol for the sea. Like many other cultures, they saw the sea as the earth's womb, a wholly feminine image.

From the days of their earliest settlements on the island, the Minoans lived by this system of matrilineal descent and female independence that many people admire even today, the same system the Minoans attributed to their deities. This social structure survived in parts of Crete long after its conquest by the Mycenaean Greeks. And just as Crete's original settlers were a group of emigrants from Asia Minor, so the Minoans continued in their desire to wander and explore. Throughout the last four millennia BCE small groups of Minoans chose to leave their island for other lands, traveling around the Mediterranean and beyond. These travels are the basis of a number of legends and myths in several different cultures.

Among the many people who claim descent from these wandering bands of Minoans are the Milesians, who ended up in Ireland. Irish legends claim a man named Miletus, a semi-divine son of Apollo (or his Minoan forebear) as their founder. According to this legend, in ancient times Miletus emigrated from Crete to Caria, in modern-day Turkey, and built the city of Miletus there. Interestingly, there is also a city called Miletus on the island of Crete. Perhaps the ancient legends reveal more than we might at first suspect.

Just as a culture grows and changes over time, so too do a religion and its practices. The Minoans' deities grew and developed as life on Crete changed over the course of several thousand years. Their goddess retained some of her earliest attributes throughout their civilization but she also changed in a number of ways.

As we can see from the deities represented as libation vessels from early Crete, the people envisioned their goddess as supporting and nourishing life through the offering of mother's milk and other liquids. This imagery continued through the time of the great temples, with priestesses pouring ritual libations and wearing clothing that revealed their breasts. But the goddess' domain enlarged beyond this mother-image as Minoan civilization became more complex.

Goddesses riding in chariots, Hagia Triada sarcophagus

When the Minoans built up their towns and began to live in a more structured society, further removed from the wilds of their island, they gave their goddess a new set of attributes. Perhaps this new emphasis served to remind the people of their simpler origins. Though they worshipped her in the towns, the goddess was the guardian and representative of nature, of the plants and animals that inhabited the island. The people adorned her altars with lilies, crocuses and other flowers. They depicted her alongside goats, birds, monkeys, even griffins. She was always shown in harmony with the creatures of nature, often feeding or petting them. We might view her as a powerful natural balance to the human-made structure and organization of the towns.

Many modern Pagans are accustomed to a goddess who has

three guises: Maiden, Mother and Crone. This European triple goddess, popularized by Robert Graves in the 20th century, was unknown to the Minoans. Their Great Goddess, regardless of her name, had two faces: the Younger and the Elder. These divisions correspond roughly to Maiden/Mother and Mother/Crone but carry slightly different connotations. Let us consider how the Younger and Elder Goddess can symbolize the stages in a woman's life.

The Younger Goddess represents the portion of a woman's life in which she has attained adulthood (is no longer a child) but is still relatively free of social responsibilities and constraints. She may or may not have children but she is still an energetic, free woman any age from young adulthood to early middle age. The woman symbolized by the Elder Goddess, in contrast, has developed the social responsibilities that come with age, experience and wisdom. Once again, she may or may not have children, but she has reached a point in her life when people depend on her for stability, assistance and advice. Different women reach this stage at different times in their lives. The Elder Goddess, therefore, represents women from middle age on into their elder years.

The Minoan God does not appear to carry the distinction of younger versus elder. In fact, almost without exception, Minoan depictions of the male deity show him as youthful and strong. He is depicted in both urban and wild settings, as is the goddess, but the god's role in nature is different from that of the female deities. The goddess is depicted among vegetation including sacred trees and flowers; any animals which accompany her are her attendants or servants but do not define her energy or her role. She is associated with growing things, with the abundance of plant life on the island. The god, in contrast, is the Lord of the Animals. Like the European Horned One, he is both the master of the animals and a part of them. In this guise he appears as the Great Stag or the Moon-Bull. These animals were not held sacred in themselves, but rather as symbols of the god. In his role as Lord of the Animals he is also the Sacred Hunter, brandishing his spear and flexing his biceps to show his dominion over the four-leggeds. In any guise, however, he is almost always youthful and strong.

The lack of an older god as a counterpart to the Elder Goddess has led some people to suggest that the god was merely a consort of the goddess with no significance apart from her. The Minoans did place extraordinary significance on their goddess in her many guises, but to minimize the god to a mere sidekick is to treat him the way the Mycenaeans treated Ariadne. The Minoan god was a powerful, vigorous figure who stood on his own to represent the virility and strength of the animal kingdom and of human men.

Symbols and Images

Let us look now at Minoan religious iconography, that is, the symbols and images the people of Crete associated with their priestesses, priests and deities. Minoan art depicts a number of different animals, plants and objects in sacred settings. These images all have specific meanings which can help us develop a stronger connection with the religion the Minoans practiced.

Although animals in general are shown with both goddesses and gods (or priestesses and priests) in Minoan art, the horned beasts and other wild creatures are representative of the god in particular in his role as Lord of the Animals. In contrast, the goddess is particularly associated with plants of various sorts since she rules over and embodies the Earth. Both indigenous and imported plants play an important role in Minoan religious symbolism. They are more often associated with female figures, both priestesses and goddesses, than male. This is perhaps due to the connection between the goddess and those things that grow in nature. While both male and female figures are associated with animals in ritual and sacrificial settings, plants appear almost exclusively with female figures.

Of the many symbols and images associated with Minoan religious settings, only a handful are human-made objects. The Minoans for the most part took their religious iconography from the natural world – plants, animals, land, sea and sky. But they also utilized items of human manufacture, most notably the labrys or double-axe. The remaining crafted items found occasionally throughout Minoan religious symbolism include other forms of weaponry. These implements were used symbolically during ritual and, in some cases, were also used for the practical purposes of ritual hunting or animal sacrifice.

The list below outlines the most common items – both natural and human-made – found in Minoan religious iconography. Some are found more frequently than others, some in particular settings only, and some at specific times during the island's history. But they all have meaning within the spiritual worldview of the people of ancient Crete.

Bird: A small but frequent image found on Minoan seal-stones, frescoes, pottery, and sarcophagi is the bird. Birds as generic figures (rather than specific species) play two distinct symbolic roles in Minoan religious iconography. First, they represent the animals with which the nature goddess is so intimately associated. Birds fly above her and cluster around her in Minoan art, showing us the connection with and affection of the goddess for her creatures. Second, birds can be messengers of the gods, much as in classical Greek mythology. We find birds perched atop columns or flying down from the heavens in ritual scenes. In these depictions, the birds send the priestesses' and priests' prayers and invocations to the gods and return from the gods with divine revelations. When an individual bird species is indicated in the artwork, it is usually a dove, eagle, hawk or crow.

Bovine Imagery: The bull holds a special place in modern interpretations of the Minoan world. We must remember, however, that many of our images of Minoan religion, particularly regarding the bull, are clouded by the Victorian-era view of history. Bovine images abound in Minoan religious art, from stylized horns to udder-shaped cups to figurines and libation pitchers. Some of these images, such as the udder-shaped cups, are unambiguously female. Others could refer to either the bull or the cow or perhaps both. We are accustomed to thinking of bulls as bearing horns and cows as being hornless, but this was not the case in the ancient world. Only in modern times have cows been polled (had their horns surgically removed) or bred to be naturally hornless as a safety measure in overcrowded farming conditions. The Minoans may well have viewed horns as symbolic of cattle in general rather than specifically bulls. Certainly, horned animals were associated with the moon and the goddess and thus were used as symbols of the divine feminine in the ancient world.

Bulls, and cows as well, inhabit an antithetical niche in the Minoan menagerie. The bull or cow is not a predatory animal, unlike the lion and eagle, so it should be seen as prey for humans and other animals. In fact, cattle were domesticated in order to provide food for humans. But cattle, especially those with horns, are dangerous beasts. They are large and heavy, with sharp horns and hooves. Bulls especially can be ill-tempered enough to attack people with no provocation. So these animals which the Minoans herded, penned and ate still struck fear (and perhaps awe) in them, enough to give them a special place in the mythical animal kingdom.

Many ancient cultures practiced the ritual sacrifice of sacred animals as a gift to the gods or as part of a communion meal with the deity to whom the animal was sacred. The Minoans, like many other Mediterranean cultures, used the blood of the sacrificed animal in special rituals as well. The blood of the Moon-

Cow or Moon-Bull was a sacred substance, considered at once life-giving and death-bringing. It was used to fertilize the fields where crops would be planted, or to fertilize the fruit trees of the vast Minoan orchards, but for a human to touch it or drink it was to risk death.

Crocus: Among the more unusual plants associated with Minoan deities is the crocus. This is one of the earliest-blooming flowers, often peeking brightly through snow to provide the first hint of spring. So, it became a special symbol of the goddess who always brought spring each year, no matter how terrible the winter may have been. As with fruits, animals, and other plants, crocuses were brought as offerings to the goddess, usually by women or, occasionally, by animals such as the monkey. Ritual participants filled the goddess' altars with crocuses and offered them to her in her form as the presiding priestess.

Dagger: The Minoans lived in a peaceful mercantile society without any military organizations, but the young men of Crete wore daggers prominently displayed at their waists. The Young God is also frequently depicted wearing a finely decorated and jeweled dagger. These blades, made of copper, bronze or silver, were ornamental and symbolic rather than utilitarian. Perhaps they were occasionally used for a more utilitarian purpose, but they were, more than anything, a status symbol and display of wealth.

The exhibition of the intricately decorated, visibly expensive dagger puts the Young God in a powerful role in a culture that valued personal wealth so highly. In a society whose Young God was often depicted wearing a prominent phallus sheath, much like medieval European codpieces, the dagger could be a further representation of his virility. The young men who wore these daggers not only displayed their affluence but also associated themselves with the Young God in so doing.

Dolphin: Dolphins occasionally appear with priests and gods in Minoan art, but the role they played in Minoan religion is one we might not find familiar. The ancient Mediterranean peoples viewed the dolphin as a marine predator and even depicted it attacking land animals. They saw it as a fierce hunter akin to the lion; it is possible that they developed this view after watching dolphins swim alongside merchant ships. Dolphins follow in the wake of ships to feed, gobbling up whole schools of small fish with their sharp teeth as the ship disturbs the fish by plowing through the water. The dolphin, then, became a symbol of the powerful priest, especially the one whose task it was to perform animal sacrifices. These graceful, powerful creatures represented the power of the sea in Minoan ritual and artwork.

Griffin: Among the mythical animals associated with Minoan deities is the fabulous griffin, an amalgamation of the lion and the eagle. A predatory and aggressive creature, it serves as a guardian to sacred figures in ancient Crete. Griffins often appear with priests and gods in Minoan art, emphasizing the predatory nature of the priest's role as sacred hunter and sacrificer. But the griffin also appears in pairs, flanking female figures – either goddesses or the priestesses who served and embodied them. In this position the fierce and fabulous creature acts as a guardian to the goddess and her priestesses, and as a marker to indicate that the person they flank is indeed a goddess and not an ordinary woman. Thus the griffins add to the power and importance of the figures they accompany. Griffins also represent the mythical aspect of nature which the goddess protects and holds dear. In Minoan art, goddess figures often feed or ride griffins, showing the deity's close affinity with this aspect of her world.

Horns: The sacred horns, usually stylized into a U-shaped ornament, sit atop shrines and temple walls to designate these places as sacred. Seal-stones also depict priestesses and goddesses wearing horned headdresses. Although we are accustomed to think of them as bull horns, the fact is that horns as a symbol of the *female* cow and of the moon are a much older sacred symbol on Crete, in Egypt and elsewhere than is the symbol of the bull. Perhaps by the end of the Minoan empire, when the cult of the Minotaur had grown quite strong, the horns came to represent this particular god and his attributes. But the sacred horns are found atop figurines from before the time of the temples, from before the rise of the great Moon-Bull on the hill at Knossos. So this particular symbol has a layered meaning in Minoan mythology. It incorporates the early Great Goddess (represented as the milk-giving cow) and her cycles of the moon as well as the later Minotaur and his bull-cult.

Labrys: The double axe or labrys is perhaps the single most recognizable sacred symbol from Crete. Though often interpreted as a weapon, in Minoan ritual it served only a symbolic purpose: it represented the divine power of the goddess. The ritual double axes that have been found at various archaeological sites are beautifully crafted and decorated, but they are too flimsy and delicate to have been used for practical purposes. The labrys is, in fact, a stylized butterfly, a symbol of the regenerative and transformative power of the goddess. This sacred tool also reflects the seasonal vegetative and agricultural cycle the Minoans associated with the goddess, for it is shaped like the hoe axes the island inhabitants used to clear land for planting. Thus again the labrys symbolizes regeneration as seen in the seasonal renewal of crops and wild plants.

In addition, the labrys is a profoundly sexual symbol. Consider the blade's resemblance to the vulva, with the labia on either side and the clitoris down the middle. This appearance makes the labrys blade a potent symbol of the feminine, both human and divine. Combine the blade with a long handle and you have a symbol of the union of male and female, the source of life itself.

We find depictions of the sacred double axe adorning the tops of shrines and ritual columns in Minoan art. When a human figure wields the labrys you may be certain it is a priestess, not a priest. The word 'labyrinth' comes from this sacred object, for it means 'House of the Double Axe.' Double axes were often placed in stands next to shrines such as the pillars in pillar crypts. They were wielded as a ceremonial representation of sacred power, much as the Egyptian pharaohs wielded the crook and flail to symbolize their sacred reign over herd and field. In many shrines and ceremonial platforms we find special labrys-stands flanking the seat of a priestess. These pyramidal stands would have elevated the labrys to the height of the priestess, lending her a greater aura of power.

Lily: The lily is a lovely flower found in the wild throughout the Mediterranean, from Spain around the coast of Asia Minor to northern Africa. It played an especially important role in Minoan religious symbology. This flower is associated with the goddess in a number of ways. We find pictures of lilies on priestesses' clothing and jewelry, even drawn or tattooed on their faces. Priestesses and supplicants offered lilies to the goddess on her altars and during rituals. These flowers filled the meadows of Crete in the springtime, reminding everyone of the beauty, abundance and fertility of their goddess. But the lily is distinct from the crocus in that its symbology has a wider interpretation. While the crocus is a specific symbol of early spring and the release from winter, the lily represents the femininity of the goddess both in her sexuality and beauty and in her maternal abundance and fertility.

Lion: One way the Minoans represented the power and strength of their deities was by flanking them with powerful animals. One of the more common of these is the lion. A number of frescoes and seal-stones depict a priestess/goddess flanked by lions, much as we might find in modern heraldry. One seal even shows a goddess riding a lion. These large, ferocious creatures provide the same guardian image as the griffin, as well as adding to the apparent power of the figures they flank. Of course, the symmetry and duplication of the same animal flanking a figure on both sides adds to the impact of the image.

Monkey: An animal you may find familiar from reproductions of the frescoes on Crete and Thera is the monkey. These creatures, depicted in blue on the wall paintings at Knossos, are often shown in botanical settings. In mythological terms they are servants of the gods and their special role is that of gatherers of the plants sacred to their patron deities. The blue monkeys at Knossos are shown gathering crocuses into baskets, perhaps to present to their goddess during a springtime ritual.

Palm: The palm, native throughout the Mediterranean countries, was a sacred tree to the people of Crete. Palm trees in Minoan art denote a sacred space in which ritual took place. Goddesses (or priestesses) are often depicted beneath palm trees. Palm trees on frescoes flanking a seat or dais indicate that a priestess, representing a goddess, would have been seated there.

Snake: One of the most powerful animal figures in the Minoan symbolic menagerie is the snake. While there are only two snake-priestess statues in existence to date, this image has come to symbolize the whole of Minoan spirituality to many people. The snake is a complex religious symbol, embodying varying and often contradictory meanings.

At its most basic level, the snake was a symbol of the under-world and of the subterranean god who later evolved into Hermes among the Greeks. The long, narrow body of the snake can be interpreted as a phallic image, reinforcing its masculine connotations. Depicting a goddess or priestess with the animal who symbolized her consort was a common artistic device in the ancient world. In addition, the snake carried connotations of renewal due to its seasonal shedding and 'rebirth.' This image of rebirth reinforces the position of the god as the underworld deity whose responsibility is the dark half of the cycle, moving from death to rebirth. Of course, as in so many human cultures, the snake also represents a power that is frightening on a very basic level, perhaps a genetic or biological response, but one that is overwhelming to many people. Thus the snake was a symbol of power and a source of awe to the Minoans both as an animal and as a deity.

A secondary association of the snake with the imagery of rebirth comes from a very early Minoan belief which still held sway even at the end of their great empire. Many early Minoans believed that when people died, their souls were freed from their bodies and metamorphosed into animals of various sorts. One of the more common of these was the snake. In fact, many Minoans apparently hoped to be reincarnated as snakes. A superstition grew up associated with the belief in animal reincarnation, that it was the karmic equivalent of murder to kill a snake. The reverence for snakes on Crete may, then, be interpreted as reverence both for the god in his underworld aspect and for the ancestors who might be reincarnated as snakes. We can see a parallel with such a belief among the Hindus, who revere cattle as both a symbol of deity and as the reincarnation of their family members. Thus they hold cattle sacred and will not harm them. The Minoans held much the same belief about snakes from their earliest settlements on the island until the collapse of their great empire.

Spear: Unlike the dagger, which is exclusively a male symbol in Minoan iconography, the spear symbolizes a deity (or person) who hunts, be they female or male. The Huntress Goddess, whose domain is the wild wood and who hunts not ordinary animals but the Stag God, carries a spear. But so, too, does the Sacred Hunter, the Young God in his guise as Lord of the Animals. Unlike the Huntress, however, the Young God hunts the wild animals who are under his dominion. When the time came for a Minoan boy's rite of passage into manhood, he would often be expected to take his spear out into the wilds of the island to hunt. This act of strength and skill linked him with the Sacred Hunter and proved his manhood to the men in his life. The spear, then, is a symbol of the act of hunting and particularly of hunting in a sacred context.

The Gods (and Goddesses) Themselves

The names by which we know the Minoan deities have come down to us filtered through the culture and language of the Mycenaean Greeks. The Greeks altered some of the deity names slightly so that they could pronounce them more easily, and some of them they translated or changed altogether. Unfortunately, we have no record of how the Minoans spoke their deities' names. In fact, we still do not understand the language they used. The few existing samples of Linear A, the writing system the Minoans used for their language, are still untranslated. We do, however, have records from some of the cultures the people of Crete traded with, Egypt among them, and these records can help us reconstruct many facets of the Minoan pantheon.

Of course, when the Greeks brought the Minoan pantheon into their own culture, they altered the original myths to fit Greek beliefs and society. We must remember that the Greeks, advanced though they may have been, were just as biased as any other society. As often happens when one culture merges with another, the beliefs of the newly dominant people change the myths of the dominated people, often to the point that the original is difficult to recognize. So it was when the dying

Minoan empire was swallowed by the newly powerful Mycenaeans. Thus we must rely on the culturally biased interpretations of the Greeks for much of our information about Minoan mythology. Subjective as they are, however, they still give us a good look at the beliefs and archetypes of the ancient Minoans.

As you move through the list of Minoan deities you may begin to feel that each goddess is simply another name for the goddess whose description you just read. You may begin to feel that each god in this list is another face of the previous god. To a certain extent this impression is correct. Early in their religious development the Minoans defined a single mother goddess, the Divine Creatrix, as the basis of their belief system. From this primal goddess grew the many faces and facets listed below. Each face of the goddess is a deity in her own right, but each face of the goddess is also just that – one aspect of the incredibly complex Great Goddess who lies at the very foundation of Minoan belief. And from this Great Goddess sprang an ancient Consort who is the root of the many faces of the Minoan gods. So, let us explore these many faces – the names, attributes and myths of the Minoan pantheon.

All deity names in **bold** type can be found in the alphabetical listings in this chapter.

Aega: Aega is a face of the primal Minoan mother goddess whose alter-ego **Amalthea** appears in the form of a goat. Aega was the mythical founder of the Aegean civilization, whose people named themselves after her. In her goat-form, Amalthea, this goddess suckled the infant god **Zagreus** in a cave on Mt. Dikte in central Crete. Zagreus' mother **Rhea** had placed him there upon his birth at midwinter in order to keep him safe. The inclusion of Aega/Amalthea in this myth established the goat as the animal totem of the early Minoans, much as the Romans drew their wolf totem from the tale of Romulus and Remus. The association of the goat with Minoan spirituality is far older than that of the bull (see **Minocapros**).

Alpheta: Ariadne, an aspect of the Minoan great goddess whom the Hellenes later mythologized into a maiden, was also called Alpheta. This name is a magical anagram or contraction, *alpha* and *eta* being the first and last letters of her name in ancient Greek. As Alpheta she was guardian of the Corona Borealis (Crown of the North) whence her consort and lover Hermes conducted souls. She lived in a silver-circled castle much like the Welsh Caer Arianrhod. The legend of Theseus and Ariadne's flight from Crete to the island of Dia, and Ariadne's wedding there to Dionysos, echoes Ariadne's identity as Alpheta. On Dia, Dionysos gave Ariadne a wedding crown which he later installed in the heavens as the Corona Borealis, to remind all people of his love for his wife.

Amalthea: She is the animal form of the goat-goddess **Aega**. According to Minoan mythology, **Zagreus** was yearly born in **Rhea**'s cave at Mt. Dikte in central Crete. He was born at midwinter like all goat kids and suckled by the divine she-goat Amalthea. Amalthea was the animal form of the goat-goddess Aega, after whom the Aegean civilizations named themselves. The story of Zagreus being suckled by a goat established the goat as the totem god of the early Minoans, just as the tale of Romulus and Remus being suckled by a she-wolf established the wolf as the totem of the early Romans. Both were hidden away soon after birth, suckled by totemic animals and raised by shepherds.

The name Zagreus can be translated as 'the torn,' meaning that he was the dismembered sacrifice. As the goat-god, yearly reborn at midwinter, he was also the communion sacrifice, seethed in Amalthea's milk in her cauldron. Being dismembered while in the Otherworld is a common experience among shamanic practitioners from ancient to modern times. Zagreus' being torn apart connects him not just with his later Greek aspect of Dionysus, but also with the earlier shamanic practices of tribal peoples around the Mediterranean and Asia Minor.

Ananke: She is the divine face of Fate or Destiny, one of **Ariadne**'s aspects as the Weaver of Life. Her name also means 'necessity.'

Aphrodite: We are familiar with Aphrodite and her later Roman counterpart Venus through the myths the Mycenaean Greeks perpetuated. The goddess' sensuality was an integral part of her personality, as was her fertility. The Greeks later separated the sensuality and sexuality from the power of the mother goddess, turning Aphrodite into a flighty, fickle love-goddess who had lost the depth and wisdom of her many-faceted predecessor. Aphrodite is in reality a face of the ancient Minoan goddess **Ariadne**. She was first and foremost a sea goddess, the source of life and fertility and holder of the Cauldron of Regeneration, the ancient sea-womb.

The Greek myth about Aphrodite's birth tells how the god **Cronos** castrated and killed his father Uranus. Cronos then threw Uranus' severed genitals into the ocean. When the blood touched the sea-foam, Aphrodite sprang from the sea fully grown. In fact, her Greek name comes from the root *aphros*, which means sea-foam. The winds bore her across the waves to the island of Cyprus, a Minoan colony and outpost of the Minoan trading empire. Aphrodite's attendants were the Seasons. Since Aphrodite is also **Urania**, we can identify her with Cronos' parent Uranus. And Cronos is a later Greek creation from an aspect of **Rhea**, the great Minoan mother goddess. Thus we see the goddess giving birth to herself from the ancient sea-womb as her blood (menstrual blood?) touches the salt-water.

The ancients saw blood as a life-giving liquid and believed that it could induce fertility, hence the reason a sacrificed animal's blood was scattered on the fields. But, in this instance, blood may be a mythical substitute for semen, since Aphrodite's birth was occasioned by the presence of male genitalia in the sea-womb. Alternately, the original myth may have specified menstrual blood as the fertilizing substance, since the deities were originally female. A later modification, changing the deities to male and adding the severed genitalia to the myth, would have satisfied the Greeks without totally obscuring the original tale.

Aphrodite is associated with the constellation Taurus whose principal (alpha) star is Aldebaran. Aphrodite rules this star, meaning to the ancients that Aldebaran represented her in the sky. Taurus also contains the Pleiades, a seven-star cluster which represents the seven pillars of Aphrodite's temple. We see similar (possibly borrowed) pillar imagery in Cabalistic belief and throughout medieval Europe. The name Pleiades comes from another of Aphrodite's names, Pleione, meaning 'Queen of the Sea.' Thus in Taurus we see the goddess standing before her temple, perhaps guarding it or beckoning her followers to it. It was said that in order to reach Aphrodite's temple one must pass the 'pearly gates' (the stars), an image borrowed by later Christianity. Does this gateway to her temple indicate the practice of astral travel among Aphrodite's followers? We may never know, but the idea, like Aphrodite herself, is quite tempting.

Arachne: Another face of **Ariadne**, Arachne is the weaver of the fates of humanity. She comes down to us through a Greek legend which describes the takeover of Minoan religion by the Greek pantheon. In the legend, Arachne (a Minoan) was such a talented spinner that she made Athena (a Greek goddess) jealous. In fact, Arachne's work was described as being beautiful to watch as she performed it, as well as attractive in the finished product. Arachne's talent was so celebrated that Athena, feeling threatened, challenged her to a spinning contest. Being so talented, Arachne easily won against the Greek goddess. Enraged, Athena turned Arachne into a spider out of spite so that all she could ever do was spin. In Ovid's version of this myth, Arachne was so sure of her own talent that she challenged the goddess to a contest rather than the other way round.

Another version of Arachne's tale speaks of a beautiful tapestry Arachne wove. It was so beautiful, in fact, that Athena went mad with jealousy and tore it up. In terror at the rampaging goddess, Arachne hanged herself. Seeing this, Athena changed her into a spider and Arachne climbed up the rope to escape the goddess' rage. This myth gives us a glimpse of a pre-Hellenic goddess who was so powerful that she could not be minimized or absorbed into the male-dominated Greek pantheon. Instead, she had to be all but obliterated by being reduced to an insect. Still, the myth lives on to this day and Arachne is not forgotten.

Ariadne: She is perhaps the best-known member of the Minoan pantheon, but she is often misunderstood or minimized in retellings of the legends from ancient Crete. Ariadne is a many-faceted deity, the primal Great Goddess in one of her many guises. She embodies both aspects of the Minoan goddess – the younger (Theseus' beloved) and the elder (the priestess of the temple). As the maiden or younger goddess she is the fresh, youthful face of the divine feminine and of her symbol, the moon. The younger Ariadne is the goddess associated with initiation and new beginnings. Ariadne does not traditionally have a consort, either in her earlier Minoan guise or her later Greek form.

As the Great Goddess whose divine presence was palpable throughout Minoan civilization, Ariadne took on many different faces and names. One of her faces as the goddess of the sea was later called **Aphrodite** by the Greeks. One of Aphrodite's pre-Hellenic titles was Fate (**Arachne** or **Ananke**) or Ariadne, weaver of the threads of life.

As primal mother-goddesses, **Rhea** and Ariadne were often used interchangeably in Minoan myths. One such instance is the tale of the birth of the god Zagreus. In some versions of the tale Rhea is Zagreus' mother. But in other versions of the tale Rhea acts in her guise as Artemis Calliste, who is the same as Ariadne. In this story the goddess placed Zagreus in a sacred cave on Mt. Dikte to hide him, then she gave him to two she-bear cubs to nurse. Here Ariadne's role is like that of Arianrhod of Celtic legend, and the two she-bears are the constellations Ursa Major and Ursa Minor. Note that the Latin constellation names have feminine endings, making them the Great She-Bear and the Little She-Bear. Mt. Dikte thus becomes the center of the sky since Ursa Major and Ursa Minor surround the Pole Star. The goddess placed Zagreus, then, in the Minoan version of Caer Arianrhod. The people of ancient Crete considered Mt. Dikte to be the sacred center or omphalos of the island and thus, spiritually, the center of the universe.

Perhaps Ariadne's most familiar role is that of the keeper of the secret of the labyrinth. Here she is the goddess of initiations and divine connection, who held the fate of mortals in her hand, the spinner of the thread of fate and weaver of the web of life. While later Mycenaean legends reduced her to a simple maiden whose task was weaving and spinning, her earlier guise was far more powerful. The thread she spun was that of each individual's path in life, their fate if they chose to follow it. We see a reflection here of her aspect as **Arachne** in the spinning of the thread that connects each of us to the divine and to each other. Ariadne's Golden Thread connects all life into the Great One. The thread can be likened to the umbilical cord linking humans to the womb-center of being. This thread led Theseus out of the labyrinth, back from ritual death to the rebirth of initiation.

Asclepius: Asclepius is the name the Greeks gave to the Minoan god of the solar year. He was born of the goddess **Rhea** Coronis, the Great Mother who holds time within herself. Asclepius was able to resurrect the dead or be resurrected from the dead: the dying and reborn god. This aspect of resurrection also includes the ability to heal many illnesses and injuries. In this way Asclepius is associated with **Hermes**, who may simply have been another Greek name for him. Asclepius, like Hermes, carried a double-serpent caduceus. These two gods share the ability to perform magical healings on those who come to them for aid.

The cock was sacred to Asclepius as the god who could resurrect the dead, just as the rooster heralds the rebirth of the day. In this aspect Asclepius was also connected with the image of the phallus through the process of dying and rising again, a symbol of virility and libido. In keeping with the symbolism of the cock, hens' eggs are dyed scarlet (the color of the blood of birth) to honor the sun as it is reborn to power in the spring. In Asclepius' other form as **Cronos** he is later sacrificed as the harvest in the autumn, only to begin the cycle anew the following spring.

Britomartis: The mother goddess **Rhea** is known by many names, among them Britomartis ('sweet virgin'), the Minoan face of Roman Diana. Bear in mind that in classical antiquity the term 'virgin' had nothing to do with an intact hymen. Instead, it referred to a woman who had left her father's house and remained on her own rather than under the protection of a husband. In mythological terms a virgin was a goddess who held her power by herself without a male consort. A virgin was, then, a young woman (mortal or divine) who chose to be without a mate. She could still be sexually active, just not married. Britomartis, like Roman Diana and Greek Artemis, was the huntress who ruled the wild wood and the creatures within it. And, like Diana and Artemis, she hunted her mate to catch him and then, at year's end, hunted him again to kill him.

Sacred to Britomartis was the **Minelathos**, the Moon-Stag whose cult antedates both the **Minocapros** (Moon-Goat) and **Minotauros** (Moon-Bull) on Crete. The stag is a royal animal who embodies male sexuality and vigor and is the oldest known symbol of the male deity. As in the Greek myth of Artemis (Roman Diana) who turns Actaeon into a stag at midsummer to love and then hunt, the Minelathos was also a year-king. This institution is familiar to us from the Celtic tradition of the Holly King/Oak King duality, wherein the old king dies at midsummer to make way for the new one. So the midsummer rite of the stag god and the huntress is the *hieros gamos,* the sacred marriage of the male and female deities that ensures ongoing fertility for the people.

Cronos: This god was created out of the cross-pollination of Minoan myth with Greek culture. In fact, Cronos was originally the great mother goddess **Rhea** herself. The intrusion into Crete of the Mycenaean Greeks gave Rhea a consort named Cronos, a variant of her own name Coronis. Coronis means 'horned,' as in the horns of the moon and perhaps, later, the horns of cattle. This name, recorded by the Scythians as Cronia, also relates the great goddess (and hence her later consort) to bovine imagery and the later bull-god cult through the meaning of 'horned.'

Rhea's Scythian name Cronia defined her as Mother Time, the imagery of the horns of the moon representing the cycles of time. Remember that the first settlers came to Crete from Scythia (Asia Minor). Rhea Cronia originally wielded the castrating moon-sickle or scythe, a Scythian weapon and implement of harvest. This is the instrument with which the god was 'reaped.' Rhea, then, was the Grim Reaper, with Cronos as her consort.

Cronos is the grain-god of the fields who is cut down at the proper time in the cycle of fertility and barrenness. He is the personification of the life-sustaining grain that must itself die in order to complete the cycle of life, death and rebirth. As the crops are reaped, the grain-god dies and returns to the earth to be born anew the following spring when the new grain sprouts. Cronos was the Father Time whom we see represented in the modern image of the old man (the old year) making way for Baby New Year. Cronos' other guise, **Asclepius**, is born anew in the spring as the year, the plants and the god renew themselves. Then as Cronos he is sacrificed in the Autumn.

While the mother goddess is the steady, constant heartbeat of the ancient earth, her consort Cronos represents the motion of the cycles. In his being we find the movement from birth through growth and eventually to death and rebirth. As Father Time he presides over the ever-shifting cycles of life, in contrast to the goddess who is the great womb from which everything is born and to which everything must return. By some accounts Cronos is said to devour his own offspring, but this tale is simply a metaphor for his embodiment of time itself. After all, everything which has a beginning, time brings to an end.

According to Robert Graves, Cronos was the grain-god of a barley cult in which human sacrifice was the rule; this was a fairly common practice in many cultures at the time. Often in ancient societies, priestesses and priests enacted the myths of their deities in order to keep in tune with the cycles of the seasons. Many cultures, perhaps Crete among them, believed that the seasonal and agricultural cycles would not continue if the proper rituals were not enacted. Graves likened Cronos to the British god Bran, who was also a sacrificial barley-king. He also suggested that the Bran cult was imported from the Aegean, perhaps from Crete itself. It is more likely that the idea of a grain-god simply moved across Europe with the spread of agriculture during the Neolithic period.

Danuna: Among the many goddesses the Minoans worshipped throughout the course of their civilization is one whose name might sound familiar. The people of Crete called her Danuna.

This name, which some scholars believe originally meant simply 'goddess,' is equivalent to the Irish Dana and Anatolian Danu and possibly to the Greek Danae, Gaulish Diana and Babylonian Dunnu as well. Perhaps these names are a remnant of the long-forgotten Stone Age goddess whose images we find in such abundance throughout Europe.

But Danuna is not just the name of a goddess. It is also the name of a tribe, the name some of the early Minoans called themselves, much as the Irish Dana is also the name of the tribe (Tuatha de Danaan means 'people of Dana'). We can use tribal goddess names such as Danuna to identify groups of people as they alternately migrated and settled, leaving the mark of their religion wherever they went. For example, toward the end of the second millennium BCE, about the time the first temples were built on Crete, a group of Minoans who worshipped the sea-goddess Amathaon migrated to Cyprus. On this island they founded the city of Amathus in honor of their goddess. And they named the island Cyprus in honor of their cult of the cypress tree, sacred to Amathaon. According to legend, these same people eventually migrated to Ireland where they called themselves the Tuatha de Danaan. A remnant of the memory of Danuna? Perhaps. No one knows for sure.

Eleithyia: This Minoan goddess, whose name comes to us intact through the Greeks, was the protector of women in childbirth. She is a midwife-goddess, helping women as they went through the initiation of risking their own lives to bring a new life into the world.

Europa: Europa is the moon-goddess aspect of the Minoan great goddess **Rhea**. Europa originated with the Minoans, and her name means *full moon* (literally, 'she of broad face'). According to legend, she was carried from Syria to Crete on Zeus' back in his form as a bull. This story echoes the original human migration of the first settlers from Syria to Crete. Europa was also the cow goddess (with horns of the moon) who was wedded to the father of gods in his form as a white bull. This form appears in the legend of the bull abducting Europa. A series of coins from the Minoan city of Gortyna shows Europa seated in a willow tree, holding a willow-basket, mating with an eagle. This suggests that her name also means 'she of the willows' (**Helice** in the later Greek pantheon), making her a sister to the goat-goddess **Amalthea**, another important member of the Minoan pantheon.

The myth of Europa's abduction describes how her children, the Minoan god-kings Minos, Sarpedon and Rhadamanthys, were fathered by Zeus. Later Hellenic Greek myth says Zeus kidnapped and raped her, but some pre-Hellenic art shows the moon-goddess triumphantly riding her victim, the sun-bull. The priestess would have sacrificed the bull as part of a sacred ceremony honoring the god. These images were later misinterpreted as the bull carrying Europa away against her will. The three children of Europa can be seen as the three phases/faces of the moon: waxing, full and waning. Europa herself is an embodiment of the moon.

Helice: The Greeks gave the name Helice, meaning the goddess of the willows, to this guise of **Europa**. The willow was among the trees sacred to the Minoan Goddess. Helice was either the sister, twin or alter-ego (depending on which version of the story you follow) of **Aega**, the ancient goddess after whom the Aegean cultures named themselves. Aega and her goat-form **Amalthea** date to the early cult of the **Minecapros** (the sacred Moon-Goat) on Crete, placing their sister Helice among the older members of the Minoan pantheon.

Hermes: Hermes is a pre-Hellenic god, though the name we know him by comes to us from the Greeks. He was one of the Aegean Great Mother's primal serpent-consorts, partaking of her wisdom because he was once a part of her. In early times his caduceus was topped with a solar/lunar disk bearing horns in the shape of snakes' heads. Hermes is strongly associated with the image of the snake or serpent. To the Minoans, the snake was a symbol of the underworld and of the subterranean god. The imagery of the snake shedding its skin in rebirth reinforces Hermes' ability to heal as well as his responsibility as Conductor of Souls (Psychopomp) from this life into the next. Among his underworld duties was the dispensation of sleep and dreams to those still alive as well as the gathering of the souls of those who had died.

Hermes' efficacy in both healing and conducting souls depended on his union with **Aphrodite** (an aspect of the Minoan great goddess) for completion, for they were two halves of a greater whole – the Hermaphrodite. As **Alpheta**, the goddess was also guardian of the Corona Borealis (Crown of the North Wind) whence her consort and sweet lover Hermes conducted souls. The two made into one became **Ouroboros**, the Great Serpent which encircles and embodies all of creation. The two serpents on Hermes' caduceus represent the intertwining of these two halves which make the whole, much as the Hindus represent the two halves of the body's energy by two serpents called Kundalini and Shakti. Early myths tell of Hermes' caduceus turning whatever it touched into gold. This is a precursor of the later tale of King Midas, a story whose lesson is that the powers of the gods are often beyond the abilities of humans to use or endure.

Hermes is associated with **Asclepius**, who may simply have been another Greek name for him. Asclepius also carried a double-serpent caduceus. Asclepius and Hermes share the ability to perform magical healings on those who come to them for aid.

Another animal associated with Hermes is the sheep. The image of the shepherd Hermes carrying a sheep on his shoulders has been found in the earliest Aegean cultures, long before the time of the Hellenic Greeks. It is possible that this shepherd imagery as well as Hermes' other traits (especially that of miraculous healings) were borrowed by the later Christians in their characterization of Christ as a healer and shepherd.

Minelathos: Sacred to **Britomartis** was this moon-stag, whose cult antedates both the **Minocapros** (Moon-Goat) and **Minotauros** (Moon-Bull) on Crete. The stag is a royal animal who embodies male sexuality and vigor and is the oldest known symbol of the male deity, represented in sculpture and painting as long ago as the Stone Age. As in the myth of Artemis who turns Actaeon into a stag at midsummer to love and then hunt, the Minelathos was also a year-king. This institution is familiar to us from the Celtic tradition as the Holly King/Oak King duality, wherein the old king dies at midsummer to make way for the new one. The midsummer rite of the stag god and the young goddess, then, is the *hieros gamos*, the sacred marriage of the male and female deities that insures ongoing fertility for the people, their land and their animals.

Minocapros: The sacred moon-goat is an early incarnation of the god **Zagreus**. Zagreus was born at midwinter, as are all goat kids, and was suckled by the goat-goddess **Amalthea**. The Minocapros was one of the earliest forms of animal totem-god revered by the Minoans. Along with the **Minelathos** or sacred moon-stag, the Minocapros pre-dated the famous **Minotauros** by many centuries. Note that all of these deities who honor the moon and consort with the moon-goddess are represented by horned animals. The horns carry the double meaning of sacred to the moon (representing the crescent phase of that celestial body) and virile (representing the libido and fertility of the animal and the god), so they are both feminine and masculine at the same time. Horns carry these double meanings in many cultures.

Minotauros: According to myth, the Minoan goddess Pasiphaë (sometimes referred to as a queen) mated with a sacred bull and gave birth to the Minotauros, whose Greek name is shortened to *Minotaur* in modern English. This legend is a mythical retelling of the *hieros gamos*, or sacred marriage, between the moon-goddess, whose attributes included horns, and her consort, who represented the virility of the island. At the height of the Minoan empire's power and wealth, ships based in Crete had bull emblems emblazoned on their sails as a symbol of their island.

During the development and growth of Minoan civilization, the Minotauros metamorphosed from an early sacrificial victim to a powerful god with a zealous following. Toward the end of the Minoan empire the Minotauros took on greater power and a monotheistic tradition grew around his worship, reminiscent of the later Mithraic cults of the Mediterranean. The Minotauros' followers even attempted to shift the whole of Minoan religion toward monotheism, with their god as the center of worship. Minoan society, however, was already beginning to crumble and the cult of the Minotauros crumbled with it.

This bull-god may be an outgrowth of a much earlier cult surrounding a particular aspect of the Minoan goddess. The moon-goddess, whose most familiar Greek name is **Europa**, bore a set of horns as a representation of the moon, whose phases were sacred to her. These horns became tied to the imagery of the cow since in ancient times all cattle, both male and female, grew horns. The cow was seen as providing life-sustaining milk, just as the goddess did, and the cow had horns, making the animal sacred to the horned moon-goddess. Early in the development of Minoan culture, the followers of this moon/cow goddess began to sacrifice bulls to their deity, especially bulls which were white like the full moon. At some point in the evolution of Minoan religion, the bull-sacrifice took on his own identity and became a deity himself, the consort or partner to the cow-goddess. It is this deity who eventually grew into the Minotauros.

The Minotauros is also closely related to the Minoan god **Zagreus**, whose name can be translated either 'the handsome bull' or 'the dismembered one.' This double meaning reminds us that the god is represented by the bull and is also ritually sacrificed according to custom. The fact that Zagreus, originally a goat-god raised by the goat-goddess **Amalthea**, later took on the attributes of a bull-god illustrates the cultural shift within Minoan society from one phase of its religion to another.

In some myths the Minotauros is depicted as a bull while on Earth during the growing season, but as a serpent during the winter when the god returned to the Underworld to regenerate. This may represent an amalgamation of the later Minotauros with the earlier goddess-consort **Hermes**, who is often seen as an Underworld serpent deity. As a potent source of fertility and vigor, the bull-god blessed the fields in annual rites. The priestesses and priests of his cult sprinkled the blood of the sacrificed bull (sometimes diluted with water to make sure it went far enough) across the prepared fields before they were planted in the spring.

It is interesting to note that the Minotauros and his labyrinth home have continued to captivate the imagination of religious minds throughout the centuries. Many medieval esotericists studied *gematria*, the system of linking words with numerical equivalents in order to discover hidden meanings. These students of the arcane often used Greek as the base language in their studies. Through this system the labyrinth (*Labyrinthos*) can be equated both with chaos (the primal state) and, interestingly enough, with foam (*aphros*). As you can see, the word for foam is the base for the goddess-name **Aphrodite** (she born of the foam). And the sea-goddess whom the Greeks later called Aphrodite was one of **Ariadne**'s many faces. So we find that the links among Ariadne's tribe continue as society grows and changes.

These medieval esotericists also studied the name of the moon-bull to find its hidden significance. Of course, they knew the Minotauros only from the heavily altered version of the myth that the Greeks spread, so they viewed him simply as a homicidal mutant in a bizarre ancient ceremony. But when they studied his name in the Greek alphabet (*Meinotauros*) they found it to be equivalent, in their sacred number system, with the sum of the word for 'bull' (*tauros*) and the word for 'lord' (*kyrios*). So through their own system of divination, these occultists discovered the significance that the moon-bull had for the ancient Minoans: he was the bull-god.

Orion: This god, known to us by his Greek name Orion, is another face of the Minoan **Zagreus**. According to myth Orion, too, was born of the goddess **Rhea**. Her milk spurting out to nourish him created the Milky Way (the Greek *rhea* means 'spurt'). He is the Youthful God, a strong and skilled hunter, much like the classical Greek Hercules, and is also Lord of the Animals.

Ouroboros: This is the Great Serpent which encircles and embodies the universe, enclosing and becoming the whole of creation. Ouroboros is created from the union of **Hermes** and **Aphrodite**, the two halves of the greater whole (hence the modern term *hermaphrodite*). The two serpents twined around Hermes' caduceus represent these two halves which, when combined, bring wholeness (healing, strength and bliss). It is interesting to note that our modern English word 'whole' is cognate to the words *heal*, *health*, and *holy*.

Pandora: One of **Rhea**'s titles as the Womb of Matter was Pandora (from Greek roots that mean *the All-Giver*). Her symbol was a huge vase or jar (*pithos*) symbolizing the source of all things, like Cerridwen's cauldron in Welsh tradition. From this vase the world and all the things in it were born, as the god is reborn from her vase every spring. The Mycenaean Greeks perverted Pandora's myth, turning her gift into a curse, with only hope left to redeem humanity. But to the Minoans, Rhea Pandora was the archetypal Great Mother, gifting the universe with her blessings.

Posidaeja: The Minoans did not recognize any masculine symbol for the sea. Like many other cultures, they saw the sea as the Earth's womb, a wholly feminine image. The Minoan Goddess Posidaeja was a personification and deification of the sea. The patriarchal Greeks, who could not comprehend such power and wisdom coming from a female deity, turned her into their god Poseidon. In the course of the transformation from goddess to god, this deity's attributes shifted from the powerful but creative feminine to the powerful, fierce, and destructive narrowly defined masculine.

Rhadamanthys: According to later Greek myth, Rhadamanthys was one of three gods or kings born of **Europa**, the moon-goddess. Some legends list the bull-god **Zagreus** (later called Dionysus) as his father. Europa's other two sons were Minos and Sarpedon, also described as being fathered by Zagreus. Rhadamanthys was so wise that in the Underworld he was made a judge of the dead. Some myths say that when he reached the Elysian Fields he married the goddess Alcmene, whose name means 'the power of the moon.' As consort to the moon-goddess, he becomes the moon-bull god like his father Zagreus. In this case he is simply another name for the bull-god, and he and Zagreus are the lover/son to the goddess, like Osiris and Horus in Egyptian mythology.

Rhea: The primordial Minoan goddesses of earth and sea were just that; they had no 'other half.' Rhea (as the Greeks called her) had no consort; she was simply Earth or Creation. She was the primordial great goddess of Bronze Age Crete and the Aegean islands. In fact, all the way up until the time of the Hellenic invasions, she was seen as the universal mother without a consort, even though other goddesses gained consorts at an earlier date. She is the Great Mother who is also the death-bringing Crone. The primal goddess embodied both gentleness and ferocity, light and dark, abundance and famine. Her dark side, so necessary to the balance of the cycles of life, was distasteful to the later Greeks and slowly dwindled to a mere memory. But the early goddess wielded great power – the power of the cycles and the seasons, the power of life and death.

Rhea Cronia (a Scythian name) was Mother Time. Remember that the first settlers came to Crete from Scythia. Rhea Cronia originally wielded the castrating moon-sickle or scythe, a Scythian weapon. This is the instrument with which the Heavenly Father was 'reaped.' Rhea, then, was the Grim Reaper, with **Cronos** as her consort. Interestingly, Cronos was originally Rhea herself. The intrusion into Crete of the mainland Greeks gave Rhea a consort whose name was a variant of her own name Coronis ('horns' as in the horns of the moon, the cycles of time) or Cronia, as the Scythians recorded it. Her name Coronis or Cronia comes from the same root as the word crone, the Indo-European root *(s)ker-* which means 'to cut.' The horns of the moon cut time into measurable pieces, just as the scythe of the crone-goddess cuts lives and the tool of the farmer cuts grain.

The Minoans believed in the never-ending cycle of birth, death and rebirth. Their mother-goddess **Rhea** accepts back in death those to whom she has given life and keeps them safe until it is time for them to return again to this world. While Rhea is the steady, constant heartbeat of the Great Mother, her consort **Cronos** represents the motion of the cycles. In his being we find the movement from birth through growth and eventually to death and rebirth. As Father Time, he presides over the ever-shifting cycles of life while Rhea as Mother Time is the great womb from which everything is born and to which everything must return.

As the primal mother goddess, Rhea is recorded in myth as giving birth to a number of different deities. She also wore a mural crown (a crown in the form of a wall) to symbolize her role as protectress of cities. Many cities in the ancient world were built within walls. These walls gave cities the imagery of being feminine, womb-symbolic places which the mother goddess protected.

Among her many maternal roles, Rhea Coronis is the virgin mother of Asclepius. One of Rhea's titles as the Womb of Matter was **Pandora** (the All-Giver). Her emblem was a huge vase symbolizing the source of all things, like Cerridwen's cauldron. From this vase the world and all the things in it were born, as the god is reborn from her womb every spring.

According to Minoan mythology, the god **Zagreus** was annually born to Rhea in her cave on Mt. Dikte in central Crete. He was born at midwinter like all goat kids and suckled by the divine she-goat Amalthea, the animal form of the goat-goddess Aega after whom the Aegean civilizations named themselves. The myth of Zagreus' birth to Rhea is the earliest dateable instance of the worship of a divine child born at midwinter in a cave. Rhea is associated specifically with Mt. Dikte in Crete but, in her form as Cybele, she lends her name to mountain caves throughout Asia Minor where such sanctuaries are called *kybela*. Thus Rhea may be considered a goddess of the mountains and of the womb-like caves within them, a view in keeping with her original scope and power as the Great Mother.

The story of Zagreus being suckled by a goat established the goat as the totem god of the early Minoans, just as the tale of Romulus and Remus being suckled by a she-wolf established the wolf as the totem of the early Romans. Both were hidden away soon after birth, suckled by totemic animals and raised by shepherds. According to ancient legend, the Milky Way was formed when Rhea's milk spurted into the sky after Zagreus' birth. The Greek word *rhea* means 'spurt of milk.' Rhea is also mentioned as **Orion**'s mother in some myths. The god whom the Greeks later called Orion can also be equated with Zagreus: according to legend Orion, too, caused the spurt of milk that created the Milky Way.

Theseus: Though technically a hero rather than a god, Theseus figures prominently in the mythology of ancient Crete and later Greece. The well-known legend of Theseus and his voyage to Crete actually dates to the Mycenaean period, long after the civilization recognizable as Minoan had ceased to exist. But this legend was built on the basis of the beliefs and practices of the Minoans as they were handed down for many generations before the encroachment of the mainland Greeks.

The legend of Theseus begins with his sea voyage to Crete from mainland Greece. His goal was to rescue the Greek youths who had been abducted to Crete as tribute to the Minoan king. Never mind that the Minoans never had a king; the Mycenaeans did and they are the ones who concocted this part of the story. The legend continues with Theseus sneaking into the palace at Knossos and befriending the maiden or servant **Ariadne**. Of course, the legend fails to mention that the palace was actually a temple and that Ariadne was the one of the names of the Minoan great goddess. In order to defeat the imaginary Minoan king and free the Greek youths, Theseus had to find his way through the maze of the labyrinth and slay the Minotauros, a ferocious creature who was half man and half bull. Theseus succeeded in his task with Ariadne's help, for she furnished him with a ball of string which marked his path into the labyrinth and thus allowed him to find his way out. But in truth, Ariadne's thread leading Theseus out of the labyrinth is the path of the ritual death and rebirth journey guided by the goddess. The cord is the umbilicus, linking humans to the womb-center of being. Interestingly, our modern English word 'clue' comes from the ancient Greek word for thread (*kliua*) by way of the Old English word for a ball of yarn (*cliewan*).

An ironic postscript to this story involves Theseus' relationship with Ariadne. He had promised to marry her, either because he fell in love with her or in exchange for her help in the labyrinth, depending on which version of the tale you encounter. The two sailed toward Greece but stopped at the island of Dia, where they and their crew disembarked. After a short stay on the island, Theseus and his crew sailed away, leaving Ariadne all alone. Some accounts suggest that Theseus left her for another woman, but others tell of Dionysus' desire for Ariadne and his threats to Theseus if he did not leave her.

The end of the tale has Dionysus appearing to Ariadne as she sits crying on the deserted shore. He comforts her and marries her, presenting her with Thetis' crown as a token of his devotion. This crown was crafted from gold set with red gems in the shape of roses by the divine smith Hephaestos. Legend states that Dionysus later set this crown out among the stars where it became the Corona Borealis (Crown of the North Wind) to remind everyone of his love for Ariadne. The Corona Borealis is one of Ariadne's attributes in her form as **Alpheta** and **Aphrodite**.

The animal sacred to Theseus is the crane, a graceful bird which bred along the shores of Crete in ancient times. The crane also gave its name to a ritual: the Crane Dance. This ritual dance drew the participants in a spiral around a horned altar, mimicking Theseus' journey into the center of the labyrinth and out again. But the dance has a double layer of meaning. On the surface it depicts the mythological tale of a boy's adventure on Crete. On a deeper level, though, it symbolizes the initiatory journey each person must make toward the center of their being and back again.

Theseus is also linked to the goat, which was sacred to the Minoans for many generations. In some myths Theseus is described as the son of Aegus, the divine goat. But the Greek sea-god Poseidon is also mentioned as Theseus' father in some tales. Bear in mind here that both Aegus and Poseidon are masculinized Greek versions of the Minoan goddesses **Aega** and **Posidaeja**. Perhaps these mentions of Theseus' male parentage are remnants of an earlier myth in which Theseus is a son of the goddess in one of her many forms.

Urania: This goddess, whose name means 'Queen of the Heavens,' is a variant name for the goddess the Greeks later called **Aphrodite**. She is therefore a face of the Minoan goddess **Ariadne**. She was first and foremost a sea goddess, the source of life and fertility and holder of the Cauldron of Regeneration, the ancient sea-womb. We can search out some clues about her true identity from a later myth involving the Greek goddess Aphrodite.

The Greek myth about Aphrodite's birth tells how the god **Cronos** castrated and killed his father Uranus. Cronos then threw Uranus' severed genitals into the ocean. When the blood touched the sea-foam, Aphrodite sprang from the sea fully grown. In fact, her Greek name comes from the root *aphros*, which means sea-foam. Since Aphrodite is also Urania, we can identify her with Cronos' parent Uranus. And Cronos is a later Greek creation from an aspect of **Rhea**, the great Minoan mother goddess. Thus we see the goddess giving birth to herself from the ancient sea-womb as the blood touches the sea.

The ancients viewed blood as a life-giving liquid and believed that it could induce fertility, hence the reason a sacrifice's blood was scattered on the fields. But in this instance, blood may be a mythical substitute for semen, since Aphrodite's birth was occasioned by the presence of male genitalia in the sea-womb. Alternately, the original myth may have specified menstrual blood as the fertilizing substance, since the deities were originally female. A later modification, changing the deities to male and adding the severed genitalia to the myth, would have satisfied the Greeks without completely obscuring the original tale.

Zagreus: The god whose name has come down to us as Dionysus, and who is sometimes conflated with Zeus, originated on Crete long before the time of the Hellenic Greeks and their Mount Olympus. In that earlier time the Minoans called him Zagreus. He is associated with two sacred animals, the bull and the goat. The myth which associates Zagreus with the bull tells how the Minoan kings (or gods, according to some accounts) Minos, Sarpedon and **Rhadamanthys** were born of the moon-goddess **Europa**, fathered by Zagreus. Later Hellenic Greek myth says Zagreus kidnapped and raped Europa, but some pre-Hellenic art shows the moon-goddess triumphantly riding her victim, the sun-bull. Minoan priestesses would have sacrificed the bull as part of a sacred ceremony honoring the god. These images were later misinterpreted as the bull carrying Europa away against her will. According to the legend, she was carried from Syria to Crete on Zagreus' back. This story echoes the original human migration of the first settlers from Syria to Crete.

The earliest evidence of worship of the Divine Child comes from Crete and links Zagreus with another animal, the sacred goat. According to Minoan mythology, Zagreus was born to **Rhea** every year in her cave at Mt. Dikte in central Crete. He was born at midwinter like all goat kids and was suckled by the divine she-goat **Amalthea,** the animal form of the goat-goddess **Aega** after whom the Aegean civilizations named themselves. The story of Zagreus being suckled by a goat established this animal as the totem god of the early Minoans, just as the tale of Romulus and Remus being suckled by a she-wolf established the wolf as the totem of the early Romans. Both were hidden away soon after birth, suckled by totemic animals and raised by shepherds. According to ancient legend, the Milky Way was formed when

Rhea's milk spurted into the sky after Zagreus' birth. The Greek word *rhea* means 'spurt of milk.' The Greek god **Orion** can also be equated with Cretan Zagreus: he, too, is reported to have caused the spurt of milk that created the Milky Way.

The name Zagreus can be translated as 'the torn,' meaning that he was the dismembered sacrifice. As the goat-god, annually reborn at midwinter, he was the communion sacrifice, seethed in Amalthea's milk in her cauldron. He later metamorphosed into a bull-god from his original goat-god form. The name Zagreus can also be translated as 'the handsome bull.' But enough of his goatiness remained that he later metamorphosed (again!) into Dionysus, whose alter-form Pan clearly shows his goat heritage. The bull-god Zagreus was a bull on earth and a serpent in his subterranean, regenerative phase. The serpent aspect links Zagreus with two other god-aspects, **Asclepius** and **Hermes**. This serpent form can also be interpreted as the god-consort we see in the famous Minoan snake priestess figurines.

Chapter 6

Ritual Overview:
The Wheel of the Year and Rites of Passage

The Collection

The rituals in the remaining two sections of the book include a year's worth of seasonal and moon rituals as well as a lifetime cycle of rites of passage. The full and new moon ceremonies and seasonal festivals are designed to be performed at specific times throughout the year. The rites of passage may be performed at any time of the year, their timing being based on the events of the participants' lives. Some of the ceremonies, particularly the New Moon rite, can be performed as solitary rituals. Others, such as the Ceremony of Marriage, are by necessity group activities. But most of the rituals can be enacted by any number of people, from a few close friends to a large gathering of participants. The most important thing is to actually perform them. While they may be inspirational to read, these rituals were designed to be enacted by you and your friends, to bring Ariadne's tribe to life and to bring healing and balance into our world.

Western European neo-paganism utilizes a year-wheel marked by eight Sabbats, the Greater and Lesser in sets of four each. Most earlier cultures, however, celebrated only four great festivals to mark the turning of the seasons, and sometimes only two or three. Our modern wheel of the year is a combination of two earlier systems, one marking the lunar cycle (the Greater or Cross-Quarters Sabbats) and another marking the solar cycle (the Lesser or Quarters Sabbats). In this cycle of Minoan-style rituals, I have stayed true to the older forms by presenting only four major seasonal holy days – a spring sun rite, a summer fertility rite, a fall harvest and thanksgiving rite, and a winter rite of release and dormancy.

The rites of passage in this collection include some which may not be familiar to members of our modern society. The more familiar ones include the Child Blessing, Betrothal, Marriage, and Memorial Rite. I have also included rites of passage that our society no longer recognizes, but which would probably have been celebrated in ancient Crete, and indeed in most cultures and societies which came before ours. When we incorporate such rites of passage into our modern lives, we acknowledge the changes and sacred cycles of our existence.

The Rite of First Blood for a girl and the Rite of Manhood for a boy are two which we would do well to reinstate, giving our young people the chance to enter formally into the society of their elders. The Initiation ceremony is a type most neo-pagans will find familiar. The Ceremony to Honor the Ancestors may also feel familiar, as it is a precursor to the European Dumb Supper and other similar rituals. One ceremony which may seem odd, however, is the Rite of Parting. Many relationships dissolve for various reasons without any formal ending in our society – friendships, marriages, and so forth. Just as the Ceremony of Marriage recognizes the formal beginning of a relationship, so the Rite of Parting recognizes and witnesses the formal ending. This ceremony is designed to make the end of the relationship official and to acknowledge the loss and grief that accompany that end, thus initiating healing for those who have severed ties.

The Details

These rituals follow a general framework that remains the same throughout the collection. I have often used the written (and thus spoken) word to delineate the sacred space for these rituals, a method familiar to most neo-pagans. The Minoans had their own method of delineating sacred space but unfortunately left no detailed record of it. Of course, they had temples and shrines where the area for religious use was marked by the building itself, but they may have performed some sort of purification of the area, much as Catholics, Buddhists and Hindus still do by censing their worship areas. As you enact these ceremonies, you may mark the ritual area with whatever method makes you comfortable. The important thing is that you are outlining the space in which the ritual will be performed, separating it from the mundane world, so your mind can focus on the sacredness of the activity at hand.

The tools used in these rituals are familiar items: goblets, daggers, spears, lengths of cord. These may be placed on an altar or elsewhere within the ritual space. The Minoans' altars – small tables of stone, plaster or wood – held food offerings, ritual tools, and cups and pitchers of wine. These altars were often set up on a small dais or platform to draw attention to them. Rather than laying their ceremonial tools on the altar as many neo-pagans do, the Minoans liked to stand them up or hang them on a wall to display them during the ritual.

One tool strongly symbolic of the Minoan belief system, an item that I have suggested for several rituals, is the labrys. This symbol has recently been revived as an emblem of the feminist movement and can be found fairly readily in the form of jewelry. It is appropriate for the priestess in any of these rituals to wear a labrys. For a more striking accent to your ritual setting, you might use a full-size labrys, either depicted through artwork (a drawing, mural, or simple sculpture) or constructed as an actual axe. The simplest method of construction, resurrected from childhood Halloween costumes, is to cut cardboard in the appropriate shape and either cover it with foil or paint it with metallic paint.

The Minoans' double axes were uniformly gold rather than silver. The ones used in formal ceremonies stood on shafts several feet long, with the axe blades themselves easily spanning two feet. Those with more ambitious inclinations might construct blades from lightweight metal and mount them on a broomstick. Remember that the labrys was a ceremonial symbol rather than a weapon; the blades need not be sharp. Remember also that the blade plus the handle symbolizes the balance of masculine and feminine together, in peaceful combination.

We know from the orientation of their temples that the Minoans found meaning in the four cardinal directions and held them sacred, though we know little about how they used this significance in their religious practice. With this in mind, I have incorporated the concept of elemental orientations into these rituals, but rather than use one of the more familiar modern orientations, I have devised an element orientation specific to the island of Crete. I have placed fire and water in the east, since most of the developed area of Crete would have had an unobstructed view of the sunrise each morning over the Mediterranean. I have placed wind in the south. The south wind blows across the island every year to herald the change from winter into spring. The Greek mainland earth looms in the north. And finally, the west is the abode of the ancestors and the gods, the place of reverence and sanctity.

Many cultures associate deities or mythological creatures with the elements, though we must remember that our standard four-element system comes from classical Greece, not Crete. For the Minoan-style arrangement I have used mythological creatures familiar to the people of ancient Crete, each one corresponding with an element whose energies the creature carries in Minoan mythology. The element of fire on Crete falls to the fantastic griffin, a powerful creature who is an amalgamation of the lion and the eagle. The griffin is a close relative of the phoenix or firebird. The element of air belongs to the sphinx, another combinatory mythical creature. This beast, imported into the Minoan pantheon from Egypt, is a combination of lion and woman, often depicted with wings. The tantalizing sphinx lives in arid regions and can die from contact with water. Water in the Minoan mythos belongs to the naiads, nymph-like creatures who live in watery caves and swim the coasts and creeks of the island. The element of earth belongs to the very earthy fauns. These mythical creatures, sometimes playful and sometimes fierce, are half goat and half human like their relative, the god Pan. The fauns are diminutive Pans, both male and female, never growing very large and always staying close to the earth.

Of these creatures, the sphinx and the naiad are traditionally female while the griffin and faun may be of either sex. Many neo-pagans utilize a system of elements in which each element is associated with either masculine or feminine energy. Rather than attempt to separate these energies between the elements, I have focused on the balance of energies within each element. The Minoans, after all, prized the balance of masculine and feminine rather than the dominance of one over the other.

Performing the Rituals

The rituals in Part Two and Part Three are based loosely on a modern neo-pagan framework that begins with the marking of sacred space, invocation of the deities, and acknowledgement of the elements. These actions are reversed at the end of each ritual, in keeping with this tradition. We do not know exactly how the Minoans performed their ceremonies, beyond the fact that the clergy acted the part of living deities and presented many of the rituals in a mystery play style. So these are not Minoan rituals, but Minoan-*style* rituals. The divine energies the people of Crete revered are quite real and will awaken for you even in a modern-style ritual, provided you take the work seriously and maintain reverence for the powers involved. Please heed my warning at the end of this section: Do not toy unduly with the rites. As written, they work well and safely.

Modern pagans participating in ceremonies and rituals may expect to sign the pentagram and light candles at the elemental and deity invocations. But the pentagram is a later European and Middle Eastern symbol and was unknown to the Minoans. It is possible they had some sign of their own, unknown to modern cultures, which served a similar purpose, but we have no evidence of such a symbol. Likewise, we have no evidence of candles used for ritual purposes. Beeswax candles were unknown to the Minoans, though they did have torches and oil lamps. Some small lamps have been found at ritual sites, but they were most likely used simply for the practical purpose of providing light. The Minoans adorned their altars with fruits, vessels of wine and small ritual tools.

Several of these rituals include a portion that I have called the Great Rite. While the term is modern, the practice is ancient. The Minoans performed symbolic and actual sacred marriages in their rituals, wedding themselves and their land with the divine. The form of symbolic Great Rite in which a male element (blade, wand, or similar symbolic tool) enters the female element (cup or bowl) is equally ancient. Many cultures across time have performed such ceremonies. In earlier ages, however, the symbolic Great Rite was most often the precursor to the sex act itself rather than a substitute for it.

In the Great Rite portions of these rituals, I have the priestess holding the feminine element and the priest wielding the masculine element. This arrangement may seem backward to modern Wiccans, particularly Gardnerians and Alexandrians, who are used to the priestess wielding the masculine element since she is the active principle. I have arranged the Great Rite this way in these ceremonies in order to more closely follow the historical precedent. The archaeological evidence we have suggests that the Minoan priestesses acted out the female portion of the symbolism and the priests, the male portion. Thus the Great Rite arrangements in these ceremonies follow the Minoan pattern.

While we have no direct evidence that a 'cakes and wine' portion of the rituals was customarily performed, the celebratory nature of many of these ceremonies certainly points in that direction. Remains of baked bread or cakes have been found at ritual sites, and the Minoans offered libations of wine on many different occasions. A number of ceremonial settings and shrines include an offering table. In Minoan art these tables are depicted bearing food, usually fruit and bread. Thus you may certainly include shared food as part of these ceremonies, as well as offering some of it to the deities you have invoked. I have not written a cakes and wine section in any of the rituals as this is a neo-pagan, and particularly Wiccan, practice. If you would like to include this activity in any of the rituals, you may place it wherever you feel it is most appropriate within the ritual framework.

If you choose, you may move the feasting to a time after the ceremony rather than during it. The Minoans enacted rituals whose main focus was a sacred meal shared with their gods and goddesses. A communal meal, with the deities from the ritual invited as honored guests, would be a fitting end to many of the ceremonies. Such an arrangement also allows for a more substantial meal at such events as a wedding or child blessing. Regardless, sweet incense and perfume, abundant fruits and plenty of sweet wine have a place in all these rituals (yes, including the Memorial Rite).

A number of these rituals involve writing something down on a piece of parchment. These days this means a piece of parchment-colored paper. The Minoans, however, did not use paper the way we do. They were familiar with papyrus through their trade with the Egyptians, but the people of Crete used clay tablets for their regular writing and record-keeping. They also used true parchment on occasion. True parchment, or vellum, is made from the skin of sheep and is as stiff as cardboard. Since true parchment is both impractical and, to some people, distasteful or unethical, parchment-style paper is a workable modern substitute.

Several of these rituals involve movement in a specific

direction around the ritual area. I have used the terms 'moonwise' and 'sunwise' to denote direction of movement. The term 'moonwise' corresponds to *widdershins* or *tuathal* and indicates movement in a counterclockwise direction. The term 'sunwise' corresponds to the expression *deosil* and indicates movement in a clockwise direction. We know that the Minoans designed their rituals to connect with and amplify the energies of the natural world. Therefore I have used directional movement in these rituals to draw upon these energies: *moonwise* for the energy of closing, releasing, ending, going inward and *sunwise* for the energy of opening, building up, expanding and moving forward.

In this set of ceremonies I have used an integrated Minoan pantheon, selecting gods and goddesses from throughout the history of the island. The choice of deities and any other distinctive portions of the rituals are explained in the notes for the individual ceremonies. I have chosen the aspects of the god and goddess that I feel are most appropriate for each occasion and I have used only deities discussed in the earlier sections of this book. Although I have given some background information regarding the deities for each ritual, you may wish to refer back to the chapter on the Minoan pantheon as you plan your ceremonies.

In these rituals, the officiants introduce themselves as the deities incarnate. This practice was common in ancient Crete. When a Minoan priestess stepped up to perform a ritual, her audience saw her as the goddess incarnate. When a woman or man puts on the garments of priestess or priest in these rites, the human becomes the deity. The priestess speaks with the voice of the goddess, the priest with the voice of the god. Only when they remove their ritual garments are they released from the presence of the deity. The Minoans truly believed that the goddesses and gods walked on Earth in the bodies of their clergy. So let the Minoan pantheon come to life within your ritual, within yourself

– and honor the Old Ones once more.

Throughout these rituals I have used the abbreviations HP and HPS to stand for High Priest and High Priestess. These terms do not refer to the leaders of any specific religious group or organization, but simply to the people officiating the ceremony. Anyone can be the High Priest or High Priestess for these rituals, whether the rituals are performed in a solitary setting, with a few friends, or in a large group.

Any of these rituals may also be performed by two same-sex officiants, providing they are willing to split the symbolic gender-energy roles between them. Some of the rituals are more easily worked with all-female or all-male clergy than others. Bear in mind, the clergy are simply stand-ins for the deities. You do not need to be in a romantic relationship with your priestly partner in order to perform a ritual together. Other rites, such as the Child Blessing, Betrothal and Marriage Ceremony are appropriate for same-sex as well as opposite-sex couples.

The assistant who performs many of the actions in these rituals would have been a younger priestess or priest in the temples of ancient Crete. The presiding priestess and priest embodied the deities during the ceremony and thus were limited in their actions. A subordinate priestess or priest would provide the narration necessary for the audience to understand the ceremony.

Many of the Minoan ritual settings, temples and shrines were designed like theaters, with a stage or dais for the ritual actions and a separate area for the audience. This arrangement gives an almost Shakespearean flavor to Minoan rituals. The assistant becomes the narrator of the play, with the priestess and priest as the players. The audience responds with set phrases and actions but does not participate to any great extent in the activity on the stage or dais. You may set up your rituals in a staged, mystery-play style setting rather than a participatory circle if you prefer. The Minoans would have been very familiar with such an arrangement.

In terms of physical setting, you may begin with the descriptions above of Minoan lifestyle, food and dress. Unfortunately for many, in addition to being costly to imitate, the most widely recognized Minoan garments are inappropriate in many public settings in our society. Just try going topless in a city park! For rites in a private setting, however, and for those with the ambition to assemble the costumes, full Minoan court regalia could be quite stunning. Refer to the books about Minoan life and archaeology listed in the bibliography for more detailed descriptions.

Central priestess, Corridor of the Processions, Knossos Temple

For those who prefer not to copy Minoan dress, simple Greek-style robes are perfectly adequate and evoke the character of the time well enough. Bear in mind that the Minoans were quite taken with fashion and appearance. Both men and women wore makeup and jewelry and styled their hair with care. Their island climate was temperate, comfortably warm through most of the year, so their garments were made of lightweight material.

The Minoans also enjoyed music in many forms, in ritual as well as in mundane settings. It is always a challenge to improvise your own music for rituals, and in case that is not feasible there are many recordings available of early music (or modern music with an ancient feel) to use in the background during your rites. Instrumental music involving flutes, drums, harps or lyres, and rattles will set the tone nicely.

Suggestions for setting, dress, decoration and accessories are included in the notes for each ritual. Feel free to diverge from these as much as your intuition and creative spirit desire. However, please do not change or substitute the deities in these rites or make other major modifications, except for the addition of a cakes and ale section as noted above. I have performed most of these rituals myself, alone or with friends, and find their forms as written to be pleasing to the forces and energies involved. Please respect the deities, and your own safety, and refrain from altering the rituals themselves. Always have a serious purpose for performing a ritual (joy and celebration count as serious purposes) and never, ever enact a ritual as a joke. You have been warned.

Let us welcome Ariadne and her tribe into our lives as we strive to enhance the balance and harmony in the world!

Part Two

The Wheel of the Year:
Moon Rites and Seasonal Festivals

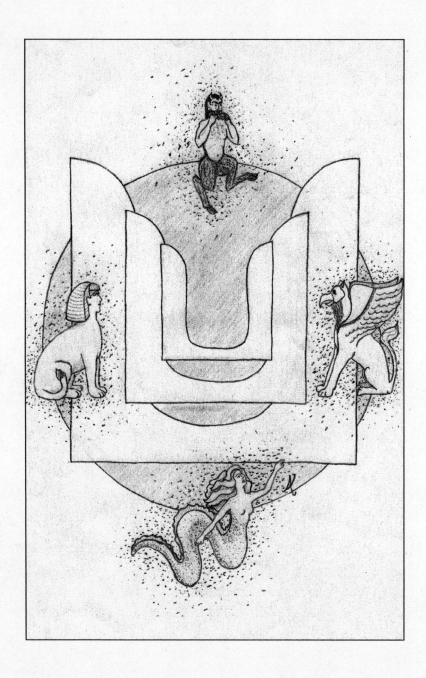

Full Moon Ritual

Europa is the moon-goddess aspect of the Minoan great goddess **Rhea**. She originated with the Minoans and her name means full moon (literally, 'she of broad face'). According to legend she was carried from Syria to Crete on **Zagreus'** back in his form as a bull. This story echoes the original human migration of the first settlers from Syria to Crete. Europa was also the cow goddess (with horns of the moon) who was wedded to the father of gods in his form as a white bull. This aspect appears in the legend of the bull abducting Europa. She is the quintessential full moon goddess, embodying the strength and the symbolism of the moon at its height of power.

This ritual is written as a framework only. The full moon is a time of serious magical workings in many forms. I have included here a marking of the sacred space, invocations of elements and deities, a symbolic Great Rite, and devocations. It is left to those performing the ceremony to insert appropriate magical workings between the invocations and the Great Rite. Remember, a ritual must always have a purpose. Do not perform this or any other ritual without a reason, even if that reason is simply celebration. Focus your energy on this reason and send the energy to it when you are done.

I suggest a simple setting for the full moon rite since the focus will be on the work being done rather than the physical surroundings. Set up a basic altar, if you wish, with your tools of choice. Put your energy into your magic. This ritual is set for two officiants (a priestess and a priest, though it may be easily adapted for two clergy of the same gender), an assistant and any number of participants. When choosing your tools for the Great Rite, it is helpful to note that the Minoans drank out of pottery or metal cups and bowls, and their blades were made of copper or bronze.

The Ritual

In a Minoan ceremony, the participants would have already gathered in the ritual area before the ceremony begins. The Priest and Priestess remain hidden until the introduction of the deities.

The Assistant indicates the boundary of the ceremonial area while speaking the following:

Between the worlds we gather now
From time and space and mind
A journey safe in goddess' womb
Till out we once more climb

Appearance of the Deities

The Assistant speaks: *Behold, the dark and light, Moon and Sun, Goddess and God – they enter to greet us!*

The HP and HPS enter and stand before the group. They look each participant in the eyes as they speak, bringing the deities into the ritual.

HPS: *I am Holy Europa, Goddess of the Full Face of the Moon, she of the dark shimmering night. By my horns you know the passing of the days and the turning of the cycles. Welcome.*

The participants bow to the goddess, acknowledging her arrival.

HP: *I am Great Zagreus, God of the Blazing Sun, he of the bright burning day. By my motions you know the passing of the seasons and the turning of the years. Welcome.*

The participants bow to the god, acknowledging his arrival.

Acknowledgement of the Elements

One of the officiants may acknowledge all the elements or they may be divided between the two, as suits them.

Officiant says to the north: *Mighty earth of the north, rugged Faun of the ancient lands, I call unto you now: Come join our rite. Bring with you the strength of the mountains, the steadfastness of rock, the power of the timelessness of life. Welcome.*

Officiant says to the east: *Blazing fire of the east, Griffin of flame, I call unto you now: Come join our rite. Bring with you the dawn of light and of passion, the power of the vigor of life. Welcome.*

Officiant says to the east: *Wide water of the east, Naiad of the deep, I call unto you now: Come join our rite. Bring with you the never-ending tides, the ceaseless rhythm of faith, the power of the womb of life. Welcome.*

Officiant says to the south: *Gentle winds of the south, ancient Sphinx of wisdom and age, I call unto you now: Come join our rite. Bring with you the breath of change, the wisdom of the skies, the power of the movement of life. Welcome.*

Officiant says to the west: *Ancient Ones of the West, those who have gone before, I call unto you now: Come join our rite. Bring with you the knowledge of life, that we are all connected, all part of the same sacred cycle. Welcome.*

At this point the HP and HPS explain the purpose of the ritual. Any serious magical workings are done, with the energy raised being directed toward the goal of the working. Any stray energy should be thoroughly grounded out.

Symbolic Great Rite

The HP and HPS may use any manageable tools they choose to symbolize the feminine and masculine energies of the universal One. The following interchange is written using the words 'cup' and 'rod.' There is some evidence that the Minoans used a realistic carved phallus for this purpose. If you use other tools, substitute the appropriate words. This symbolic rite may be the beginning of a food and drink portion of the ritual. If this is the case, have the cup filled with the sacramental wine before you begin. Otherwise, the empty vessel stands as a powerful symbol of the goddess, the womb waiting to receive both the beginning and the end of life.

The HPS holds the cup up in front of her. The HP holds the rod above it. As they begin to speak, the HP lowers the rod into the cup. They alternate lines, speaking the last line together.

HP: *As the rod is to the male*

HPS: *So the cup is to the female*

HP: *God to Goddess*

HPS: *Priest to Priestess*

HP: *Man to Woman*

HPS: *They come together, two into One*

HP: *And their union brings into the world*

Both: *Fulfillment, beauty and love.*

Food and drink may be shared if this is a part of your ritual. Otherwise it is time to bid farewell to the forces you invited into your ritual.

Farewell to the Elements

The officiant who invoked each element now bids farewell to that same element.

Officiant says to the west: *Ancient Ones of the West, those who have gone before, we thank you for your presence in our rite, for your wisdom and guidance. We bid you now return whence you came with our thanks. Farewell.*

Officiant says to the south: *Gentle Winds of the South, ancient Sphinx of wisdom and age, we thank you for your presence in our rite, for your wisdom and motion. We bid you now return whence you came with our thanks. Farewell.*

Officiant says to the east: *Wide Water of the East, Naiad of the deep, we thank you for your presence in our rite, for your rhythm and constancy. We bid you now return whence you came with our thanks. Farewell.*

Officiant says to the east: *Blazing Fire of the East, Griffin of flame, we thank you for your presence in our rite, for your passion and vigor. We bid you now return whence you came with our thanks. Farewell.*

Officiant says to the north: *Mighty Earth of the North, rugged*

Faun of the ancient lands, we thank you for your presence in our rite, for your strength and steadfastness. We bid you now return whence you came with our thanks. Farewell.

Farewell to the Deities

The Assistant bids farewell to the deities: *Great Zagreus, God of the Blazing Sun, we thank you for your presence in our rite. We will always remember your strength and your brilliance. Farewell.*

The HP steps out of view.

Assistant: *Holy Europa, Goddess of the Full Face of the Moon, we thank you for your presence in our rite. We will always remember your strength and your loving embrace. Farewell.*

The HPS steps out of view.

The Assistant returns the ritual space to the mundane world:

Take down the walls and open the door
From placeless space and endless time
The sacred space shall be no more
From goddess' womb we now do climb.

The rite is ended.

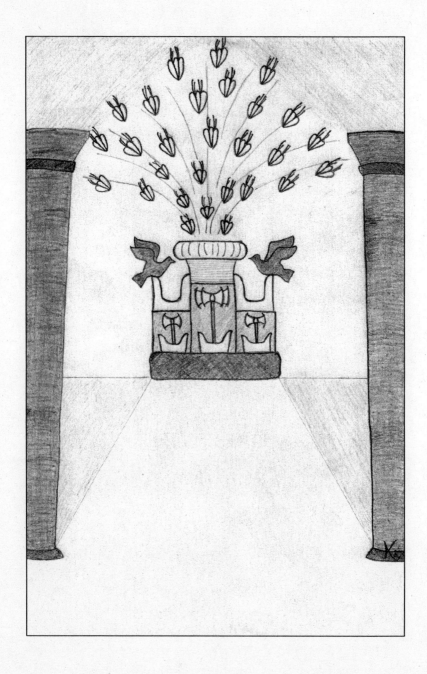

New Moon Ritual

The lovely **Ariadne** embodies the energy of the moon, and as the maiden she is the youthful and new face of the goddess. Ariadne is the deity associated with initiation and so is appropriate as the goddess aspect for a new moon ritual, especially one in which new beginnings are made. She does not traditionally have a consort and for this ritual I have left her alone as the only deity invoked.

The new moon is a time of strong female power and is traditionally the time when women menstruate, the menstrual period historically being referred to as 'moon-dark courses' or 'dark-moontime.' In a number of cultures, the time of the new moon is a time for the women to go off among themselves. In our society this time can also be seen as an opportunity for each person, male or female, to look within, release the old and make a new start in any aspect of his or her life.

For this ritual I have used the image of a temple rather than the labyrinth so often associated with Ariadne; that potent symbol and place is reserved for the Initiation ceremony in Part Three. Ariadne is the goddess of new beginnings: make your new beginnings in her temple and in your heart.

This ritual is designed as a solitary act. While there are ways of making new beginnings within a group of people, the new moon is a good time for solitary workings; even the goddess turns her face within.

Have your ritual area set up as you feel comfortable. Make sure you will have no distractions (turn off the phone, lock the door, send the kids to the movies, etc.). For the strongest psychological effect you need a dark ritual area. If you perform this ceremony during the day, you will need to darken the room. If your blinds or curtains are not thick enough, you may need to drape a sheet or blanket over the window. Dress as you feel comfortable. Remember that even though you are alone, this is still a formal ritual, so change out of your daily clothing. If you are comfortable doing so, perform the ritual skyclad. Your 'birthday suit' is always appropriate attire for new beginnings; after all, it's how you began this life.

As a symbol of transformation and regeneration, the labrys is an appropriate tool for this ritual. Whether worn as jewelry or displayed above the altar, it will remind you of your goal and reinforce the purpose of renewal.

Set up your altar at one end of the room with your favorite tools and accessories. Place a small table or other stable surface at the end of the room opposite your altar. You will need two small oil lamps (candles will do) for this ritual. Be sure the ritual area will remain undisturbed for as long as it takes all the lamps to burn completely out. If you do not have a particularly private ritual area, you may move the lamps to a safe place when the rite is over, but do not extinguish them. Please never leave burning oil lamps or candles unattended. It is amazing how mischievous cats and small children can be, so BE CAREFUL!

Instead of beeswax or paraffin candles, the Minoans used small oil lamps made of pottery or metal, shaped like a bowl or small pitcher. Many of them looked like what we think of as Aladdin's magic lamp. They did not look like modern oil lamps, the upright sort with a base that holds the oil and a glass globe over the flame. Whatever light source you choose, it needs to be small enough to handle and transfer across the room easily without worry of spilling or breakage. I will use the term 'lamp' throughout the ritual for continuity. If you choose a different light source, simply substitute that word.

Before the ritual, meditate on how you will make a new beginning. Choose carefully what you will be leaving behind and what you will be taking on anew. State these two things clearly in a few words. You may write these two things down on small pieces of parchment. Put the piece of parchment with the old that you are giving up on the altar and put the other parchment, with the new that you will be taking on, on the second table before you begin.

The Ritual

Place one of the lamps, unlit, on your altar. Place the other lamp (also unlit) on the opposite table.

Mark the sacred space for your ritual, saying:

I cast about with ancient Art
The Temple of the Goddess true
Whose essence lives within my heart
Whose presence lets me start anew

Acknowledgment of the Elements

Acknowledge the elements.

Say to the north: *Mighty Earth of the North, rugged Faun of the ancient lands, I call unto you now: Come join my rite. Bring with you the depth that receives the old back to its source, and the strength and steadfastness to carry on with the new. Welcome.*

Say to the east: *Blazing Fire of the East, powerful Griffin of flame, I call unto you now: Come join my rite. Bring with you the dawn, the flame that burns away the old, that cleanses to make way for the new. Welcome.*

Say to the east: *Wide Water of the East, shimmering Naiad of the deep, I call unto you now: Come join my rite. Bring with you the tides that sweep away the old, the rain that brings freshness. Welcome.*

Say to the south: *Gentle Winds of the South, ancient Sphinx of wisdom and age, I call unto you now: Come join my rite. Bring with you the breath of change, the breeze that clears the air and blows away the old. Welcome.*

Say to the west: *Ancient Ones of the West, those who have gone before, I call unto you now: Come join my rite. Bring with you the knowledge of the web of life, that sacred strand that connects us all. Welcome.*

Call to the Goddess

Call upon the goddess: *Ariadne of the Golden Thread, young and fair and new, I call unto you: Come join my rite. Bring with you the silken thread that is the fate of all living, that with your help I may find the next step on the path of my life. I thank you for your presence and your power. Welcome.*

Light the lamp on the altar, saying: *I light the Temple with the flame of my being. I fill the Temple with my will. Tonight I return a portion of myself to the Temple, that I may make room for the new to arise within me.*

Now you will perform the magic of the ritual, returning something old to the Temple to make room for something new in your life. Focus on the flame until you have reached a meditative state. Concentrate on that which you have chosen to leave behind. State it aloud in the same words you have written on the parchment.

Burn the parchment in the flame, saying: *I consign the old to the flames, that it may return whence it came. I return it to the Temple.*

To return it to the Temple, pick up the lit lamp and carry it across the room to the opposite table. Use it to light the new lamp.

Snuff out the old lamp, saying: *The Temple has received the old, which I return. Now I bring out the new.*

Focus on the new flame. Concentrate on that which you have chosen to begin. State it aloud in the same words you have written on the parchment.

Burn the parchment in the flame, saying: *I bring the new into being. I awaken it with fire.*

Carry the new lamp back to the altar.

Focus on the flame, saying: *I bring the new out of the Temple and into my life. As the flame burns, my purpose and my new beginning grow stronger.*

Do not extinguish the lamp. Meditate on the changes you have made in this ritual and how you will blend them into the rest of your life.

Farewell to the Goddess

Thank the goddess and bid her farewell: *Ariadne of the Golden Thread, young and fair and new, I thank you for your presence in my rite. In your Temple I have laid down the old and have taken up the new, that I may continue on my journey down my life path. I thank you for your presence and your power. Farewell.*

Farewell to the Elements

Thank the elements and bid them farewell.

Say to the west: *Ancient Ones of the West, those who have gone before, I thank you for your presence in my rite, for the knowledge of connection with all things. Return now whence you came. Farewell.*

Say to the east: *Blazing Fire of the East, powerful Griffin of flame, I thank you for your presence in my rite, for the cleansing flame, the fire of the new dawn. Return now whence you came. Farewell.*

Say to the east: *Wide Water of the East, shimmering Naiad of the deep, I thank you for your presence in my rite, for the washing waters and the refreshing rain. Return now whence you came. Farewell.*

Say to the south: *Gentle Winds of the South, ancient Sphinx of wisdom and age, I thank you for your presence in my rite, for the breath of change and the clearing breeze. Return now whence you came. Farewell.*

Say to the north: *Mighty Earth of the North, rugged Faun of the ancient lands, I thank you for your presence in my rite, for the enveloping depths and your strength and steadfastness. Return now whence you came. Farewell.*

Return the ritual space to the mundane world, saying:
The Temple built by ancient art
Remains forever in my heart;
The sacred space where work was done
Returns now to the greater One.

Leave the lit lamp to burn itself out. You may relight the other lamp from this one and let it burn down as well, consuming the old to make way for the new.

Spring Sun Festival

Asclepius is a god of the solar year. He is also the deity who is able to resurrect the dead or to be resurrected from the dead: the dying and reborn god. One of his animal emblems is the cock, a symbol of resurrection since it heralds each day's new dawn. In keeping with the symbolism of the cock, hens' eggs are dyed scarlet (the color of the blood of birth) to honor the sun as it is reborn to power every spring. In Asclepius' other form as **Cronos**, he is later sacrificed as the harvest in the fall. But now he is resurrected as the earth is reborn from winter into spring.

Rhea Coronis is the virgin mother of Asclepius. One of Rhea's titles as the Womb of Matter was **Pandora** (the All-Giver). Her emblem was a huge vase symbolizing the source of all things, like Cerridwen's cauldron. From this vase the world and all the things in it were born, as the god is reborn from her womb every spring.

This ceremony celebrates the hatching out of the world. The officiants include a Priestess, Priest and Assistant. It would be appropriate for the Priestess of this ceremony to be pregnant. However, if she is pregnant, practice the ritual carefully to make sure that the birthing scene does not induce premature labor in her. The Priestess may dress as she likes, but her skirt should reach her ankles in order to hide the bowl of eggs and the HP as he moves out from under the altar. The HP should be dressed scantily. If the participants are uncomfortable with nudity, he may wear a small wrap or short skirt. The effect should be that of 'Mother-naked', the way we are all born.

The ritual area should be gaily decorated, perhaps with bright spring flowers and ribbons. The altar should contain symbols of spring – lilies and crocuses, if available, other flowers and perhaps the first fresh fruit of the season. There should be a bowl or other large unbreakable vessel in front of the altar. Be sure it is large enough to contain all the eggs the participants will bring into the ritual. The altar needs to be a table or other piece of furniture that is tall enough for the HP to crawl under. Drape it to the ground with a colorful cloth. This is a festive occasion, not at all solemn unless you consider birth a solemn event.

The participants gather in the ritual area. Each one carries an egg dyed bright red, a gift for the god of spring. The HP is hidden under the altar table before the participants arrive. The HPS is elsewhere within the ritual area, out of sight of the participants.

The Ritual

The Assistant marks the ritual space according to his or her way, bearing in mind that it will be the womb which contains life for time of the ritual.

Appearance of the Deities

The Assistant calls upon the goddess: *Great Mother Rhea, Pandora the giver of all things, I call unto you: Come now that we may witness the mother as she brings life anew to the world. Come that we may praise you and rejoice in your love.*

The HPS steps into view and speaks: *I am here among you now. Let us celebrate the return of the spring and the rebirth of life from my womb.*

The participants bow to the goddess, acknowledging her arrival.

The Assistant goes to each participant in turn, asking them: *Who seeks to celebrate the return of life from the Womb of Matter from which all things are born?*

Each participant responds: *I am [insert name]. I bear a gift, a hen's egg red as birthing blood. I await the birth of spring.*

The Assistant welcomes each participant and motions them toward the HPS, who stands with her bowl before the altar. The HPS speaks to each one in turn.

HPS: *Behold the Womb of Matter, the vessel of Pandora the All-*

Giver from whom all creation comes. Place your gift within the bowl, that you may be one with the new life that comes to us today.

She motions the participants to place their eggs in the bowl. They then return to their places around the ritual area, facing the altar. The HPS places the bowl of eggs on the floor, against the front of the altar.

The HPS then tells the story of the dying and reborn god. While she speaks, the HP is hidden under the altar. The HPS stands in front of the bowl of eggs as she speaks.

HPS: *Hear now the story of the Great Circle of Life. I am the Great Mother who gives birth to all things. But all things, once born, must also die that they may be born anew. So it is with the God of the Fields. For he grows throughout the summer in the fertile earth, washed by the rain and warmed by the sun's rays. He grows great and strong and fills the fields. And when the sun begins to dim and a chill touches the once-warm air, he calls his people to him, for this is the time of harvest. He gives himself to his people that they may live and flourish, that they may have food in their bellies during the long, cold winter.*

As the HPS continues to tell the story, she backs up toward the altar so that her skirt covers the bowl of eggs.

HPS: *So the grain is harvested, the god is sacrificed. He returns then to me, the Great Mother, where he waits. He waits for the sun to grow bright again, for the air to warm and the earth to awaken. And so it has: feel the warm sun upon you, the earth ready to begin again that great cycle which we celebrate today. And so life begins again, as it always has and always will, with a birth: the birth of the new god, the dawning of Life!*

The HPS may cry out as if in labor. When he is ready, the HP taps her leg or gives some other pre-arranged signal. HPS spreads her legs and lifts her robe. HP spills the red-dyed eggs from the bowl between HPS's legs in imitation of the shower of birth-blood. Then he crawls through her legs, being born anew into the world. He stands up and gives the cock's crow of dawn.

All the participants shout together: *The dawn of new life!*

Spring is here! The god is reborn!

The participants all join hands in a circle around the HP and HPS. They sing and chant and dance in a circle. Food and drink may be shared here as a part of the ritual or a celebratory meal may take place after the ritual has concluded. Once the singing and dancing have wound down it is time to conclude the ritual.

Farewell to the Deities

The Assistant bids farewell to the deities: *Asclepius, the newborn god, Lord of the Dawn, accept our gracious thanks for your return to us. You bring with you life, green and growing. May you grow ever stronger through the year as the wheel of life turns. Now return to your dwelling place with our gratitude and love.*

The HP retreats out of sight.

Assistant: *Great Mother Rhea whose cauldron is the womb whence all things are born, accept our gracious thanks for your presence here today. You are the beginning of all life and the end to which all life must return. Now return to your dwelling place with our gratitude and love.*

The HPS steps out of sight.

The Assistant returns the ritual space to the mundane world, saying: *As the womb is opened for birth into new life, so the sacred space is opened that we may all be reborn to the new life of Spring. Let us go forth now into the world to live and grow in love.*

The rite is ended.

Summer Fertility Festival

Rhea is known by many names, among them **Britomartis** ('sweet virgin'), the Minoan face of Roman Diana. Bear in mind that in classical antiquity the term 'virgin' had nothing to do with an intact hymen. Instead, it referred to a woman who had left her father's house and remained on her own rather than under the protection of a husband. In mythical terms, a virgin was a goddess who ruled in her own power without a consort. A virgin was, then, a young woman (mundane or divine) who chose to be without a mate. She could still be sexually active, depending on the culture and society, just not married.

Sacred to Britomartis was the **Minelathos**, the moon-stag whose cult antedates both the **Minocapros** (moon-goat) and **Minotauros** (moon-bull) on Crete. The stag is a royal animal who embodies male sexuality and vigor and is the oldest known symbol of the male deity. As in the myth of Artemis, who turns Actaeon into a stag at midsummer to love and then hunt, the Minelathos was also a year-king. This institution is familiar to us in the Celtic tradition of the Holly King/Oak King duality wherein the old king dies at midsummer to make way for the new one. So the midsummer rite of the stag god and the young goddess is the *hieros gamos*, the sacred marriage of the male and female deities that insures ongoing fertility (of womb, family, garden, and wallet, as applicable and desired) for the people.

This ritual takes place outdoors in an area such as a field, pasture or large backyard. There is a small enclosed pavilion or tent toward the east end of the ritual area. The altar is set up in the center with symbols of the fields (green plants, grain, etc.) and of the stag (antlers, figurines and such). A cup filled with red wine is hidden beneath the altar.

In addition to an officiant (priestess or priest) this ritual calls for two men to play the two aspects of the Stag God and a woman to play the Huntress. The men dress in rustic garb (rough brown cloth, woodland-style) or animal skins. The first Minelathos wears a headdress of deer antlers. The Huntress wears a short tunic and sandals or soft boots. She carries a spear. Drums, rattles and other musical instruments are appropriate in this rite.

The participants gather in front of the altar before the sacred space is marked. The Huntress and the first Minelathos are in the pavilion, out of sight before the participants arrive. The second Minelathos stands among the participants, trying to be inconspicuous.

The Ritual

Officiant marks the ritual space, a wide space that encloses the participants and the pavilion and leaves a good deal of room around them as well.

Appearance of the Deities

The officiant calls upon the goddess: *Hail Britomartis, bright shining one, huntress of the moon. Come to us now, swift of foot, strong and sure, sweet Lady. Show us your shining face.*

The Huntress steps out of the pavilion and stands in front of it. The participants bow to her, acknowledging her arrival.

The officiant calls upon the god: *Hail Minelathos, great horned one, stag of the moon. Come to us now, swift of foot, strong and sure, robust Lord. Show us your woodland face.*

The Minelathos steps out of the pavilion and stands in front of it, next to the Huntress. The participants bow to him, acknowledging his arrival. The officiant tells the participants the story of Britomartis and the stag while the Huntress and Minelathos act out the story.

Officiant: *Now is the height of the summer; the fields are full with the ripening grain; the vines are heavy with sweet grapes. The Goddess has had her consort, has kept him by her side and loved him. She has had* *her fill of his company and now she yearns for the hunt.*

The Huntress shoves the Minelathos away, urging him to run from her. He trots a short distance away and waits.

Officiant: *The Huntress scents the Stag on the wind. Long has she lain in comfort, resting. Now she stretches and rises and makes ready. The time has come.*

The Huntress stretches, hefts her spear and turns toward the Minelathos. She has the menacing look of the hungry hunter. He is frightened and begins to run away from her, around the circle, moonwise. She chases him. They run near the edge of the circle, around the altar and participants. They run moonwise around the circle, the Huntress chasing the Stag, while the story continues.

Officiant: *The Minelathos, the great Moon-Stag, is now the hunted one. His virility awakened the goddess and the earth to the fertility and abundance of midsummer. Now the fields are full and the consort has served his purpose. He must return whence he came. The Huntress chases, as she must. Her desire spurs her on and she will not rest until she has captured her prey.*

Everyone watches as the Huntress and Stag finish their chase. The Minelathos staggers toward the altar in exhaustion. He collapses in front of the altar, completely at the Huntress' mercy. She stands poised over him with her spear. The officiant continues to narrate.

Officiant: *The quarry is caught. The consort gives himself up to the goddess and the earth, that his body may nourish the growth he has initiated. He must return whence he came.*

The Huntress sinks her spear into the ground behind the stag in such a way that she appears to have speared him. He shudders and dies. She crumples to the ground next to him, grieving. The officiant takes the cup of wine from beneath the altar, as if taking it from within the stag. She holds it up for all to see and speaks.

Officiant: *The blood of the Moon-Stag nourishes the earth that the fields may fill to overflowing.*

The officiant sprinkles some of the wine on the ground.

Officiant: *Share now in this nourishment wrought from great sacrifice, that your lives may fill to overflowing with abundance and joy.*

The officiant blesses each participant with the wine. S/he may either sprinkle it over them in the ancient gesture of blessing, or mark each one on the forehead with the wine.

When everyone has received the blessing, the narration continues: *The Huntress grieves. For though she has brought down her quarry, now she is alone. Her consort is no more.*

The second Minelathos steps out of the crowd and walks up toward the altar. He kneels at the head of the fallen Stag and removes the antler headdress. He puts the antlers on his own head and stands tall and proud as the new Minelathos.

Officiant: *Out of the old rises the new. The Great Stag lives!*

The Huntress sees the new Minelathos and moves toward him, as if hunting him, but without her spear. The Minelathos backs away and begins to run. The Huntress chases the Minelathos sunwise around the circle as the story continues.

Officiant: *The Huntress again sights her quarry, but now she hunts from the heart. Her desire spurs her on and she will not rest until she has captured her prey.*

The Huntress and Stag finish their chase in front of the pavilion. The stag collapses in exhaustion. The Huntress stands over him.

The officiant narrates: *The quarry is caught. The consort gives himself up to the Goddess, that the cycle of growth and fertility may continue.*

The Huntress grabs the Stag and drags him into the pavilion, passion and desire clear on her face. While the participants have their attention on the pavilion, the fallen Stag gets up. He goes quietly to a prearranged place out of sight of the ritual attendees, removing himself from the ritual space if necessary.

The participants drum, chant and dance in the ritual area in celebration of the continuing cycle of the land, allowing their energy to flow off toward the purpose of fertility of all sorts. When all is quiet again, the ceremony continues. The Huntress and Stag emerge from the pavilion and stand in front of it, just as the Huntress and Minelathos stood when the deities were invoked.

The officiant speaks: *Out of the old rises the new, the goddess and the god ever changing and ever still the same. So, too, does the earth grow green and flourish, then die away to cold barrenness, only to return anew to the green. Let us revere the great cycle of life and rejoice in it. And let us give thanks to the Huntress and the Stag.*

Farewell to the Deities

The officiant bids farewell to the Minelathos: *Minelathos, great horned one, stag of the moon, we thank you for your presence in our rite and in our lives. We bid you now return to your dwelling place with our gratitude and our love.*

The Minelathos steps into the pavilion.

The officiant bids farewell to Britomartis: *Britomartis, bright shining one, huntress of the moon, we thank you for your presence in our rite and in our lives. We bid you now return to your dwelling place with our gratitude and love.*

The Huntress steps into the pavilion.

The officiant returns the sacred space to the mundane world then speaks:

The wheel has turned. The rite is done.

All the gods' blessings on everyone!

There may be music and dancing afterward, and perhaps food (or at least wine). Once the ritual is over, the man who played the fallen Stag may reappear, but he should change clothes so as not to be seen in the Minelathos costume.

Autumn Harvest Festival

This ritual is similar in nature to the harvest ceremonies enacted throughout Europe and the Mediterranean until just a century or two ago. The main focus is thanksgiving for the bountiful harvest, the grain of which is also the sacrifice of the grain-god for the sustenance of his people. The goddess is seen here as **Rhea**, the great mother who is also the death-bringing crone. Her consort **Cronos** is the god of the fields, the personification of the life-sustaining grain that must itself die in order to complete the cycle of life, death and rebirth.

Rhea Cronia (a Scythian name) was Mother Time. Remember that the first settlers came to Crete from Scythia. She originally wielded the castrating moon-sickle or scythe, a Scythian weapon. This is the instrument with which the Heavenly Father was 'reaped.' Rhea, then, was the Grim Reaper, with Cronos as her consort. In his other guise as **Asclepius**, he is born anew in the spring, and as Cronos he is now sacrificed in the autumn.

Interestingly, Cronos was originally Rhea herself. The intrusion into Crete of the mainland Greeks gave Rhea a consort named Cronos, a variant of her own name Coronis ('horns' as in the horns of the moon, the cycles of time) or Cronia, as the Scythians called her. Cronos was the grain-god of a barley cult in which human sacrifice was the rule (not particularly uncommon given the time). Cronos is likened to the British god Bran, who was also a sacrificial barley-king and whose cult was imported from the Aegean, perhaps from Crete itself, according to Robert Graves.

This rite is to be enacted after the last harvest is gathered. The ritual area is prepared out-of-doors if possible, the ritual to take place at sunset or after dark. There should be a large fire in the center of the circle which will be built into a bonfire at the close of the ritual. At least two people must remain to tend this fire until dawn (or until it goes out, whichever happens first). Torches outline the circle area. The darker the surroundings, the more intense the effect.

There are bound sheaves of barley or some other grain standing around the ritual area and one unbound sheaf lying on the altar. Traditionally, the unbound sheaf would be the very last grain gathered at the end of harvest. Standing against the altar is a full-size scythe, preferably a real one (available from feed stores, garden supply stores and the like). On the altar also sits a flagon of dark red wine and a loaf of coarse bread, made from the newly-harvested grain, if possible.

Any decorations, altar cloths and such should be black, red or gold. The color black represents the elder/death aspect of the goddess and the formless space between death and rebirth. Red represents the blood of the god, spilled to nourish the earth, returned to the earth whence it came. Gold represents the wealth of the fields, the golden-ripe grain which sustains the life of those who grow it. Thus gold is also the color of the god.

Appropriate incense would be any of the embalming resins: myrrh, sandalwood, frankincense. If you choose to use incense, have enough on hand to keep a good strong scent in the air from the very beginning of the ritual. Incense powder sprinkled on the central fire is an easy way to develop a strong scent.

Dress should be darkly celebratory. This is not a somber occasion, though it is serious. The priest may be dressed in gold (metallic, even). The priestess, as the Grim Reaper, should be dressed darkly, but perhaps with a golden face.

Those who wish to participate must bring with them either a small flammable item or something they have written on parchment representing what they wish to consign to the flames as a sacrifice. They must also have in mind the chief thing for which they give thanks.

The Ritual

The participants are already gathered in the ritual area. The HP and HPS are hidden near the altar. The Assistant marks the sacred space in his/her chosen way.

Appearance of the Deities

The Assistant calls to the deities. As s/he invokes each one, the HPS and HP step out where they can be seen.

The Assistant calls first to the goddess: *I call unto you, Rhea Cronia, Mother of Time – come now unto us. Bring us your strength and your wisdom for the task at hand. Bring us the knowledge of the circle that holds all circles, everywhere and nowhere found, the Great Circle of existence itself.*

HPS: *I am here.*

The Assistant calls to the god: *I call unto you, Cronos, King of the Fields – come unto us. Bring us your golden youth and abundant virility for the task at hand. Bring us the knowledge of the cycle within the cycles, the endless circle of birth, death and return, the Great Circle of existence itself.*

HP: *I am here.*

The HPS addresses those gathered around. While she speaks, the HP quietly goes to the altar and picks up the unbound sheaf of grain, holding it against himself as if it were a part of him.

HPS: *We are gathered here to give thanks for the bounty of harvest. The grain is gathered, our storehouses are full, the young god has given his energy and vitality that we might all grow strong in the abundance of the earth. The earth has poured out her life that we might flourish. Now we pour out a symbol of our life, wine red as blood, in gracious thanks to the Great Mother.*

The HPS picks up the flagon of red wine and shows it to the people. She holds the flagon high in one hand and pours the wine out onto the palm of her other hand, the blood-red wine flowing between her fingers and down to the earth at her feet, then she speaks.

HPS: *Holy Rhea, mother of us all, we offer you a sacrifice this night. Each person here has tasted your abundance, known your plenty. And so we each give back to you something we hold dear. Accept these, our tokens of gratitude as we return to the earth a symbol of what we have taken.*

The HPS goes around to each participant and questions them: *Who seeks to enter the circle of fire out of the darkness of night?*

The participant gives his/her name.

HPS: *Do you bring the price, a sacrifice dear to you?*

Participant: *Yes.*

HPS: *Then bring also your thanksgiving and step into the circle of fire.*

The HPS directs the participants to step up to the central fire. Each person should reflect briefly on the sacrifice they will make, then place the object or slip of parchment in the fire. When everyone has offered their sacrifice to the fire and returned to their place, the HPS speaks again.

HPS: *Great Mother, Rhea Coronis, we give thanks to you for your great abundance. And we give thanks also to your son and consort Cronos, King of the Fields, for though the earth gives her plenty, the god gives his life that we may also live.*

The HPS replaces the flagon on the altar and bows to the HP, acknowledging his sovereignty. The HP steps forward and speaks, as a king speaking to his people whom he loves. As he speaks, he may walk around the circle, looking each person in the eye.

HP: *I am the bounty of the land, the food of the fields that sustains your life, the harvest you celebrate today. But I am more still. I am the culmination of the cycle of life, the circle of life: the fulfillment of your plans, the fruit of your labors, ripe and ready for picking. And as you have given of yourselves that you may reap a harvest, now I offer myself to you as the Lord of the Fields. You must take my life that yours may continue. This is the way of all things. For all plants are born, grow, and die, to return to the earth whence they are reborn; so too must all the* *living return to the mother to be born anew.*

Here is the mystery: all life is one life. In order to receive we must also give. It is time for the harvest, time to reap the bounty, time to take what is yours. Know that the fruits of the earth are freely given to you who revere them. Know that the sacrifice is made freely and with love.

The HP holds the unbound sheaf of grain upright in front of him, as an extension of himself. He kneels before the HPS.

HP: *I give my life that all may live. I shall live again.*

The HPS cuts the sheaf in half with the scythe, being careful not to cut the HP in half (though this would be a historically accurate act). The HP drops the cut grain onto the ground. The HP may then either lie on the ground in front of the altar, as if dead, or step into hiding somewhere in the ritual area.

All: *The king is dead. He will come again in his time.*

The HPS gathers the reaped grain from the ground and throws it into the central bonfire. She returns the scythe to the altar and retrieves the bread and the remaining wine. She pours the wine into a goblet and holds it up for all to see.

HPS: *The wine we drink is the life-blood of the grape. Let us share it in thanksgiving for the creatures and plants that nourish us.*

Everyone present passes the cup around the circle, each person giving the next a drink. Then the HPS holds up the loaf of coarse bread and breaks it.

HPS: *The bread we eat is the body of the grain god, given freely in harvest to us. Let us share it in thanksgiving for the creatures and plants that nourish us.*

Everyone present passes the bread around the circle, each person giving the next a small piece to eat. When all have shared bread and wine, any remaining wine is poured out on the ground as a libation to Rhea. Any remaining bread is given to the fire.

HPS: *What has been given, we have taken in gratitude and love. Let us give thanks for the bounty of the god and goddess as we enjoy the harvest throughout the winter months. Let us remember what is given* *up, that we may have what we need.*

Farewell to the Deities

If the HP is still visible in the circle, the Assistant may gesture to his body as s/he speaks the devocation.

Assistant: *Cronos is dead, sacrificed to the needs of the hungry. But his spirit lives, to be born once again when the warm spring comes. Cronos, we thank you for your sacrifice, the greatest giving. Depart now to your dwelling place to await the springtime and your new dawning. Blessings upon holy Cronos!*

If the HP is still lying on the ground, two or more participants pick him up (as if he were dead) and carry him away where he cannot be seen.

The Assistant bids farewell to the goddess: *Rhea Cronia has reaped the harvest and taken back to her what is hers. Mother Time, goddess of the Great Circle, the never-ending cycle, we thank you for your presence tonight. We bid you depart now to your dwelling place with our gratitude and love. Blessings upon holy Rhea!*

The HPS steps out of view. The Assistant then returns the ritual space to the mundane world. There may be music and dancing around the bonfire after the ritual is over. Especially, young men may add grain stalks to their clothes and dance in circles around the fire in imitation of the cycle of life in the fields. The bonfire needs to be allowed to burn out or be put out before dawn. Of course, for safety's sake, the fire should never be left unattended.

Midwinter Festival

The earliest evidence of worship of the Divine Child comes from Crete. According to Minoan mythology, **Zagreus** was newly born each year in **Rhea**'s cave at Mt. Dikte in central Crete. He was born at midwinter like all goat kids and suckled by the divine she-goat **Amalthea**. Amalthea was the animal form of the goat-goddess **Aega** after whom the Aegean civilizations named themselves.

The story of Zagreus being suckled by a goat established the goat as the totem god of the early Minoans, just as the tale of Romulus and Remus being suckled by a she-wolf established the wolf as the totem of the early Romans. Both were hidden away soon after birth, suckled by totemic animals and raised by shepherds. According to legend, the Milky Way was formed when Rhea's milk spurted into the sky after Zagreus' birth. The Greek word *rhea* means 'spurt of milk.' The Greek god **Orion** can also be equated with Zagreus because according to legend he, too, caused the spurt of milk that created the Milky Way.

The Minoan cult of the moon-goat, the **Minecapros**, was far older than the bull cult which eventually grew up around the **Minotauros**. Aega, the human form of the goat-goddess Amalthea, was the sister, twin or alter-ego (depending on which legend you prefer) of the goddess **Helice**. The name Helice means 'willow', a tree sacred to the Minoan goddess. Helice was later described as either the consort or the daughter of the king of Crete, much as the Minotauros was eventually called the king or son of the king of Crete.

Helice is associated with the sacred willow tree which, according to Pliny, grew outside the cave on Mt. Dikte where Rhea bore Zagreus. In another version of the tale, Rhea in her guise as Artemis Calliste placed Zagreus in the cave on Mt. Dikte to hide him. Then she gave him to two she-bear cubs to nurse. Artemis Calliste can be interpreted as Ariadne/Arianrhod and the two she-bears as Ursa Major and Ursa Minor. If this is the case, then Mt. Dikte becomes the center of the sky, since Ursa Major and Ursa Minor surround the Pole Star. Rhea placed Zagreus, then, in the Minoan version of Caer Arianrhod. The Minoans considered Mt. Dikte to be the sacred center, or *omphalos*, of their island.

Zagreus later metamorphosed into a bull-god from his original goat-god form. The name Zagreus can be translated as 'the handsome bull.' But enough of his goatiness remained that he later metamorphosed (again!) into Dionysus, whose alter-form Pan clearly shows his goat heritage. The bull-god Zagreus was a bull on earth and a serpent in his subterranean, regenerative phase. This serpent form may very well be the god-consort we see in the famous snake priestess figurines.

The name Zagreus can also be translated as 'the torn,' meaning that he was the dismembered sacrifice. As the goat-god, yearly reborn at midwinter, he was also the communion sacrifice, seethed in Amalthea's milk in her cauldron.

Midwinter is a time of dormancy. Little can be done to move ahead: no crop can be sown or harvested, no ground can be prepared. Remember your grandmother darning socks by the fireplace? About all you can do at midwinter, cooped up inside to avoid the cold, is repair those things which have been damaged in the previous seasons and put them away to await the spring. This ritual allows us to put away those things we can't do anything about right now, until the time is right to bring them out, just as Rhea put Zagreus into the cave on Mt. Dikte until the time was right to bring him out.

In preparation for this ritual, think about those things which you have been unable to let rest even though you can do nothing about them just now. These things take up your energy and fill your mind when you need to put your concentration elsewhere. Now is the time to set them aside; not throw them away, but put them somewhere safe until the time comes to get them out again and deal with them. When you have thought about what you need to put away, write these things down on a small piece of parchment. Put the energy of your thoughts, frustrations and worries into the words as you write them. Bring the parchment with you to the ritual.

The ritual should take place late at night; the time of day should match the time of the season. The ritual area may be arranged as you usually do, with one addition: a cave. A table draped to the floor with a dark cloth would be suitable. The 'cave' needs to be big enough for an adult to crawl under easily. Under this table place a basin full of dirt. The container should be big enough for everyone to put their pieces of parchment into and cover them over with soil. On the altar, in addition to your chosen tools and accessories, have a cup of milk large enough for all to share and an uncut loaf of bread.

The Ritual

The HPS and HP are hidden from view as the ritual begins. The participants stand within the ritual area as the Assistant marks the edge of the ritual space around them, thus enclosing them as if in a cave.

The Assistant says:
Between the worlds I take us now
From time and space and mind
A journey safe in goddess' womb
Till out we once more climb

Appearance of the Deities

The Assistant calls to the goddess: *I call unto you, Rhea, great mother of all. Come now unto us. Bring us your strength, your wisdom and your deep faith. Bring us all the knowledge of the circle that holds all circles, everywhere and nowhere found, the great circle of existence itself.*

The HPS steps into view and speaks.

HPS: *I am here.*

The Assistant calls to the god: *I call unto you, Zagreus, divine child, son of the great mother. Come now unto us. Bring us your fresh youth and newness. Bring us all the knowledge of the cycle within the cycles, the endless circle of birth, death and return, the great circle of existence itself.*

The HP steps into view and speaks.

HP: *I am here.*

The participants make themselves comfortable around the ritual area before the HPS speaks.

HPS: *I am the great mother who gives birth to all that is. Tonight, the longest, darkest night of the year, I have brought forth the new god that the cycle of life might continue. But now is still the dark time, the winter, with its short days that pass quickly into long, bleak, cold nights. So I must hide my child. I must keep him safe and protected within the womb of the cave so that he may emerge healthy and strong when the time comes.*

The HP steps forward.

HP: *I am the new god, the newborn year. Newly emerged from the womb of the mother, I must now pause within the earth, for my time has not yet come. Now is the time of waiting, of setting aside that which cannot yet be finished. Everything has its own time and we must each recognize this within our own lives.*

You have each brought with you into this circle something which waits, some part of your life whose time has not yet come. It is indeed hard to wait, but patience is a part of wisdom. Think now on that which you will put to rest. Think about why you must put it down. Think about the fact that the right time has not yet come.

[Pause.]

Now is the time for putting away, for waiting. My mother Rhea bore me at midwinter and hid me safe in a cave that I might remain and grow until the time came for me to emerge into the world. Within this space lies my cave. Within the cave is a mystery. And the mystery is this: that everything comes in its own time. No matter how much we may wish it otherwise, we can no more bring time faster than we can hold the wind in our hands. So give me these things that must wait. I will keep them safe for you in my cave until it is time to bring them out again.

The HP may choose to crouch within the cave, or he may sit at the mouth of the cave to guard its entrance. Alternately, in imitation of Minoan art, he may sit atop the cave as the goat (and hence the god) is shown doing in a number of frescoes and seals. Provided, of course, the table is strong enough to support him. The HPS then leads each participant in turn to the mouth of the cave.

HPS (to each participant): *Bury the paper deep within the earth and with it bury the need to hurry. Within the cave there is no time, only being.*

Each participant crawls into the cave and buries his/her parchment in the container of dirt. He/she then returns to the rest of the participants. When all have entered the cave, the ritual continues with the sharing of food. HPS holds up the milk and bread and speaks.

HPS: *You see before you that which sustains life from generation to generation: the milk that makes the babe grow strong and the grain that nourishes those already grown. Let us share them now among us, that we give thanks for the gifts of life.*

The HPS offers milk and a small piece of bread to the HP and to each participant around the ritual area. When all have had a share, she gives the milk and bread to the participant closest to her. The remainder is passed from person to person until it is gone.

Before the end of the ritual, the HP explains what is to be done with the materials in Zagreus' cave.

HP: *Those things you have buried deep within my cave, I will keep safe for you. Wait with patience and you will know when their time has come. When it is time, come to me and I will return to you what you have given me for safekeeping. Then may you act upon it in your life,* *in its proper time.*

The HP will keep the container of dirt which holds the participants' pieces of parchment. When each participant feels the time is right, he/she will ask the HP to return the parchment. Then the participant can take action regarding what had been waiting. When all have asked for the return of their slips of parchment, the HP returns the dirt to the ground. If, by the next midwinter, there are still pieces of parchment remaining, the HP may remind the owners of this fact. If they do not want the parchment back the HP may bury them when he returns the dirt to the Earth.

It is likely that some of the participants will never ask for their slips of parchment. Many will discover that the thing they have put away in the cave needed to be left alone to work itself out without disturbance. The HP may discuss this fact individually with the participants when he offers to return the parchment.

Farewell to the Deities

The Assistant bids farewell to the goddess: *We thank you, Rhea, great mother of all, for your presence in our circle tonight, for your strength, your wisdom and your deep faith. We bid you return to your dwelling place with our gratitude and love. Blessed be Rhea!*

The HPS steps out of view.

The Assistant bids farewell to the god: *We thank you, Zagreus, divine child, son of the great mother, for your presence in our circle tonight, for your fresh youth and newness. We bid you return to your dwelling place with our gratitude and love. Blessed be Zagreus!*

The HP steps out of sight.

The Assistant returns the ritual space to the mundane world, saying:

Take down the walls and open the door
From edgeless space and endless time
The sacred space shall be no more
From goddess' womb we now do climb.

The rite is ended.

Part Three

Rites of Passage:
From Birth to Death and Beyond

The Blessing of a New Child

One of **Rhea**'s titles as the Womb of Matter was **Pandora** (the All-Giver). Her emblem was a huge vase symbolizing the source of all things, like Cerridwen's cauldron. To the Minoans, Rhea was the archetypal great mother, the creator-goddess of all that is. Originally she had no consort, but for this ritual we will pair her with her later partner **Cronos**.

Hellenic invasions from the Greek mainland gave Rhea the consort Cronos, a designation which is a variant of her own name Coronis, which means 'horned' (as in the horns of the moon). Cronos then became Father Time, partner to Rhea Coronis as Mother Time.

If possible, hold this ritual outside in a place where the rising sun can be seen as it clears the horizon. At the seashore or in a meadow would be ideal, but even a backyard can be a lovely and appropriate setting. The ritual area should be decorated as for a festival, for this is a joyous occasion. Flowers, flower petals and ribbons would be appropriate. Playing some quiet, happy music on a portable stereo will add to the effect. A gathering with food and drink following the ceremony is in keeping with Minoan tradition. This ritual is appropriate for children of same-sex couples and opposite-sex couples. It is also a lovely way to welcome an adopted child into the family.

The site is prepared: an altar at one end of the ritual area, on which are placed a piece of incense-type charcoal, a chalice of sea-water (or salt water), a bird's wing (or feathered fan) and a container of soil. Be sure to remember either matches or a lighter, to light the charcoal. There should also be a container of incense powder, chosen and given by the child's parents or god/dess parents. This incense will be blessed for the child, to be used in rituals for him or her from now on. Perhaps it could be a special blend just for the child, the first gift from the god/dess parents.

The Ritual

The participants gather within the ritual area. There are two Priestesses, one for each aspect of the goddess (younger and elder), and one Priest. All three are hidden from view as the ritual begins. The Assistant marks the ritual space in his/her preferred manner.

Appearance of the Deities

The Assistant then calls to the goddess in her two forms, younger and elder:

Oh great Rhea, come to meet us
For a new life comes to greet us;
Let us cherish in our hearts
The greater whole, the many parts;
Younger Goddess, Elder One,
Come and make your presence known.

The two Priestesses step into view.

The Assistant calls to the god:

Cronos, come and join us here
In this otherworldly sphere;
Come and bless this newborn one,
Father Time, Consort and Son.

The Priest steps into view. The parents come forward with their child and any god/dess parents who are present. They stand in front of the altar with the Priest and Priestesses, where the participants can see them as they enact the following.

Priest: *Witness now the magic and the blessing of the gods, the union of the elements and divinity that brings forth life.*

Elder Priestess: *Here is the earth whence we all come and whither we must all return.*

She picks up the pot of soil and shows it to the participants. She then places the pot prominently on the altar where everyone can see it.

Younger Priestess: *Here is the water which nourishes life.*

She pours the water from the chalice into the pot of soil.

Priest: *Here is the fire which is the spark of life.*

He lights the charcoal and places it on top of the wet soil in the pot.

Parent: [One or both parents may speak.] *Here is the wind which is the breath of life.*

One or both parents use the wing or fan to fan the coal until it glows with heat. The parents now step forward with their child. The god/dess parents present the child's incense.

God/dess parents: *And here is the mystery, the love of humans, the love of the gods, the unfathomable touch of divinity that brings forth life into the universe.*

They place a pinch of the incense on the charcoal.

As the smoke begins to rise, the Priest and Priestesses say together: *Witness the beginning, the conjoining of the elements that rise from waiting into being, into that most sacred and precious of all mysteries, life itself.*

The parents and god/dess parents present the child to the participants.

The Priest and Priestesses announce the child to the people.

Priest and Priestesses: *Welcome, [child's name], to the community of life. May you always know the love of the gods from whom you have come. May we always see and remember the divine within you.*

The parents take the child around the circle, introducing him or her to each participant. Each participant should welcome the child by his or her name. Each may also give the child a blessing.

Farewell to the Deities

The Assistant bids farewell to the god:

Father Time, Consort, and Son,
Our rite of mystery is done.
We thank you for your divine grace
And bid you return to your dwelling place.

The Priest steps out of view.

The Assistant bids farewell to the goddess in her two guises, younger and elder:

Rhea, Young and Elder One,
Our rite of mystery is done.
We thank you for your divine grace
And bid you return to your dwelling place.

The two Priestesses step out of view. The Assistant returns the ritual space to the mundane world. The rite is ended. A celebratory gathering afterward would be appropriate.

Rite of First Blood

The Minoan goddess of initiations is **Ariadne**. Her golden thread connects all life into the great One. She is both the younger goddess (Theseus' beloved) and the elder goddess (the priestess of the temple) and so represents the link between maidenhood and womanhood as a girl grows into a young woman. Of course, for this ceremony there is no male deity invoked.

A portion of this ritual is taken from a series of frescoes on the island of Thera, a Minoan colony and trading outpost in the eastern Mediterranean. This artwork depicts the puberty rite of a young woman on the island. Her tasks include traversing rocky terrain barefoot in order to pick crocus flowers sacred to the goddess. She must then present these flowers to the priestess who is, according to Minoan belief, the goddess incarnate during the time of the ritual.

This ceremony is a celebration of a girl's initiation into the mystery of the woman's body and menstrual cycles. It takes place as soon as possible after she has begun to menstruate. For the ritual itself, the celebrant and the women in her life go off to a private setting – in the woods or perhaps in someone's backyard – away from everyone else. When the ritual is over, all the participants then return to a party given in the girl's honor, with her family and friends in attendance.

If the ritual is to take place outdoors, the site should be near an area of blooming flowers. They need not be crocuses; flowers in general represent the goddess and the blooming of a girl into womanhood. If the time of year or an indoor site precludes any flowers growing nearby, preparation for the ceremony should include placing flowers nearby on the ground as if they were growing there. The area of flowers should be outside the marked ritual space. There should also be a large bunch of flowers hidden within the ritual area. There should be enough blooms for each participant to have at least one or two.

If possible, the celebrant's mother should priestess this rite. Otherwise, the officiant should be a woman who fulfills a maternal role in the young woman's life. The assistant should be an older woman, someone the celebrant looks up to. The participants are women, young and old, who are a part of the celebrant's life. Those in attendance should all have already reached menarche.

The celebrant brings to the circle a symbol of her childhood – a toy, child's book, or similar item – which she will give up during the ritual. The participants each bring a small gift which to them symbolizes womanhood, or a poem or story that tells of the riches of life as a woman. This is also the time for the young woman's mother to announce to her the things she will now be allowed to do, such as get her ears pierced, wear makeup, or some other privilege agreed upon beforehand by her parents.

For this ritual there is no need for an altar or other trappings, though you may use them if you like. You will, however, need a chair to use as the goddess' throne. It may also be a good idea to provide seating for the participants, particularly if some of them are elderly or have health conditions which prevent them from standing for a long period of time. If you do provide extra seating, be sure the goddess' throne stands out as special and separate from the other chairs.

This ceremony is an appropriate setting for the young woman to take on a ritual name. If she will take a new name during the ceremony, her teachers should discuss this with her beforehand. The name may be one of her own choosing or one that is given to her, depending on her family's traditions. If she is to adopt a new name during the ritual, she will use that name when she introduces herself to the goddess. Her given name should be inserted in the blanks in the ritual up to that point, after which she should be referred to by her new name.

As a time of transformation, the Rite of First Blood is an

appropriate setting for the symbolic labrys. A large labrys standing up next to the goddess' throne would be a striking visual reinforcement of the energy of the ritual. The labrys, worn as jewelry or as decoration on clothing, is appropriate adornment not only for the priestess but also for the participants and the celebrant as well.

The Ritual

The participants gather in the ritual area before the ceremony begins. The HPS is out of sight; she will be given a special seat (the goddess' throne) which sets her apart from the others when she appears. The young woman whose first blood is being celebrated sits or stands near this seat.

The Assistant marks the ritual space around all the participants, saying:

Between the worlds I take us now
From time and space and mind
A journey safe in goddess' womb
Till out we once more climb

Appearance of the Goddess

The Assistant leads the celebrant to the center of the ritual area and calls to the goddess.

Assistant: *Holy Ariadne, weaver of the golden web, spinner of the golden thread that binds us all into one, we call unto you now: come join us in celebration of the growth of (_____) toward womanhood. As you are both the younger and the elder, so too does (_____) stand on the threshold between two worlds. Come and be with us as we celebrate the life of woman, the realm of goddess. Welcome.*

The HPS steps into view but does not sit down. She stands at the front of the group, with the celebrant next to her. The HPS announces the purpose of the ritual by introducing the celebrant to the participants.

HPS: *We gather together in the sacred circle to celebrate the time of* *new womanhood for (____). This is a time of new beginnings for her and of a new understanding of the cycles of the moon and of the woman's body. To acknowledge her growth into womanhood, a growth toward maturity, I will introduce her anew to the elements.*

Acknowledgment of the Elements

The HPS takes the celebrant by the hand and leads her to each direction as she acknowledges the elements.

The HPs says to the north: *Mighty earth, body of the mother, come now to us as we celebrate the growth of (____) into a young woman. Bring her the patience of the ageless earth, the steadfast and sure wisdom of the land. Welcome.*

The HPs says to the east: *Fire of dawn, blushing sunrise, come now to us as we celebrate the growth of (____) into a young woman. Bring her your passion, your fervor, the awakening warmth of growth and understanding. Welcome.*

The HPs says to the east: *Wide waters, deep sea-womb of the mother, come now to us as we celebrate the growth of (____) into a young woman. Bring her your faith, your knowledge of the rhythm of the tides and the cycles of life. Welcome.*

The HPs says to the south: *Gentle wind, breath of the mother, come now to us as we celebrate the growth of (____) into a young woman. Bring her the freshness of the cool breeze that blows away the old to prepare for the new. Welcome.*

The HPs says to the west: *Ancient ones, wise women of our past, come now to us as we celebrate the growth of (____) into a young woman. Bring her your wisdom, the history of womankind from the time of the first birth. Welcome.*

The Initiation

The HPS explains the purpose of the ritual.

HPS: *Today we come together as a family of women to celebrate the advent of womanhood in (____). For ages upon ages we have celebrated this time in the life of the young woman, a time of growth and new*

*understanding. (_____) has begun to learn about her body. She will
also learn about her changing role within the family and within society,
for this is a time of transformation in a young woman's life. It is the
beginning of a new life, the life of a woman no longer a child. As with
any initiation, for each young woman this time is different. But here is
the mystery: though each of us walks her own path in her own way, we
all walk the path of the goddess. Let us celebrate the goddess in our
bodies and in our lives as we celebrate the time of first blood for
(_____).*

The celebrant shows everyone the item she has brought which
she will give up. She tells its significance, how it symbolizes her
childhood, some aspect of her life which she is leaving behind as
she grows up. She gives it to the HPS in safekeeping, perhaps
until such time as she will wish it back to give to her own child
(or she can arrange beforehand to get the item back after the
ceremony, if it something of great significance to her).

The HPS speaks to the celebrant: *(_____), you have shown us
by giving up the (token of her childhood) that you are no longer a child.
Now you must show us that you are, indeed, a woman. Your task is a
simple one, but one with much significance.*

*As a child you have watched the rituals, learned about the goddess,
and listened to your elders. As a woman you must now perform the
ritual yourself. Here is what you must do.*

[The HPS motions to the flowers growing or placed nearby.]

*Here are the blooms sacred to the goddess, the glowing blossoms of
unfolding life. You must gather these blooms in your arms and bring
them to the temple, to the throne of the goddess. Present them to her and
present yourself to her as well. For now that you are a woman, you have
a place and a duty in the temple.*

The celebrant must remove herself from the ritual space to
gather the flowers. She should do this according to the method
her spiritual family uses, perhaps by cutting a doorway in the
'wall' of the sacred space. As the celebrant gathers her flowers
the women may quietly hum or chant in the background. While

the celebrant is outside the ritual space, HPS seats herself on the goddess' throne and all the participants turn to face her. When the celebrant has an armload of flowers she must return to the ritual space.

The celebrant must bring the flowers into the ritual area and present them to the goddess (the HPS), laying them at her feet. The young woman may bow or kneel out of respect for the goddess. The celebrant then introduces herself to the goddess by her name, either her birth name or a chosen new name, and places herself in the goddess' service. There is no set phraseology for this part, as the young woman must speak from her heart.

Once the celebrant has presented herself to the goddess, the HPS rises and speaks to her.

HPS: *Welcome, (_____), to the Temple of Woman. As you take a woman's place within your family and within society, so too do you take a woman's place in the temple. And the place of woman is also the place of the goddess. Take, then, the place of the goddess and feel her power and love within you.*

The HPS motions for the celebrant to take the priestess' throne. The other participants take the flowers that have been hidden in the ritual area, distributing them equally among themselves. Each participant approaches the celebrant just as the celebrant approached the HPS, acknowledging her as the goddess incarnate.

The participants say to the celebrant: *As the spark of the divine lives within us all, you are truly the goddess, today and every day.*

Each woman in the circle tells the celebrant some aspect of womanhood that has meaning and importance to her. Each woman also gives the celebrant a small gift: a blessing, a piece of poetry, a small object which to her symbolizes the mystery of the female.

Once all the participants have presented themselves to the celebrant-as-goddess, the ritual takes on a less formal tone. This is the time for her to ask questions of the women gathered with her. This is an appropriate time for an open and frank discussion about sexuality and the responsibility that goes with it, and other issues which will confront the celebrant as she enters the world of woman.

Farewell to the Elements

The HPS bids farewell to the elements.

The HPs says to the north: *Mighty earth, body of the mother, we thank you for your presence here, for the patience of the ageless earth, the steadfast and sure wisdom of the land. We bid you now return to your dwelling place, with our gratitude and love.*

The HPs says to the east: *Fire of dawn, blushing sunrise, we thank you for your presence here, for your passion, your fervor, the awakening warmth of growth and understanding. We bid you now return to your dwelling place, with our gratitude and love.*

The HPs says to the east: *Wide waters, deep sea-womb of the mother, we thank you for your presence here, for your faith, your knowledge of the rhythm of the tides and the cycles of life. We bid you now return to your dwelling place, with our gratitude and love.*

The HPs says to the south: *Gentle wind, breath of the mother, we thank you for your presence here, for the freshness of the cool breeze that blows away the old to prepare for the new. We bid you now return to your dwelling place, with our gratitude and love.*

The HPs says to the west: *Ancient ones, wise women of our past, we thank you for your presence here, for your wisdom and the knowledge of the long and sacred history of which we are the newest part. We bid you new return to your dwelling place, with our gratitude and love.*

Farewell to the Goddess

The Assistant bids farewell to the goddess: *Holy Ariadne, weaver of the golden web, spinner of the golden thread that binds us all into one, we thank you for your presence at our celebration of the growth of (_____) toward womanhood. We thank you for the spark of the divine* *that rests within us all, for just as we are a part of you, so are you a part of each of us. We bid you now return to your dwelling place, with our gratitude and love.*

The HPS steps out of view.

The Assistant returns the ritual space to the mundane world, saying:

Take down the walls and open the door
From edgeless space and endless time
The sacred space shall be no more
From goddess' womb we now do climb.

After the ritual is over, the women bring the celebrant back to a party in her honor. The rite is ended but the journey is just begun.

Rite of Manhood

The rite of manhood is a ceremony common to many cultures around the world and throughout time. It celebrates the changing of a boy into a man and his earning of certain rights and privileges as he grows older. Many cultures include an ordeal, either symbolic or real, as the proof that the boy has achieved strength and courage and thus, manhood. This ritual involves a symbolic ordeal, a test of trust for the young man as he enters the community of adult males. The deity here is **Minotauros** who is strong, wise and virile. Of course, there is no goddess invoked.

The men in the celebrant's life are the participants in his Rite of Manhood, preferably with his father (or a father figure) as the High Priest. The rite is to be held in a secluded place, perhaps outdoors. The celebrant's parents should decide ahead of time what privilege he will be given during the ceremony. It would be appropriate to have a party arranged to begin when the ritual ends.

This ceremony is an appropriate time for the young man to take on a ritual name. If he will take a new name during the ceremony, his teachers should discuss this with him beforehand. The name may be one of his own choosing or one that is given to him, depending on his family's traditions. If he is to take a new name during the ritual, he will announce that name at the appropriate time. His given name should be inserted in the blanks in the ritual up to that point, after which he should be referred to by his new name.

Contests or displays of physical prowess were common in Minoan male rites of passage. Among the most frequent of these were hunting and fishing. The boy to be initiated would set out to hunt or fish, either alone or with an older man (perhaps his father) in order to prove his strength and cunning. Later during the rite, the postulant would present the animals he had caught or killed, displaying them before all the participants and perhaps arraying them on the altar.

If your personal philosophy allows for such activities, an overnight hunting or fishing trip in the wilderness would be an appropriate prelude to the Rite of Manhood. Even without the hunting or fishing, a night spent alone in the woods would be an ordeal similar to those of many different cultures. Always remember, though, to take adequate safety precautions and have an experienced adult available within a reasonable distance. The ordeal should end in the ritual, not the emergency room.

There is no need for an altar for this ritual, although a table set with symbolic masculine objects (horns, acorns, and so forth) would be appropriate. If the rite is to take place outdoors, be sure the area is fairly level and free of obstacles. There should be a sturdy tree trunk, table or similar object about waist-high to the celebrant placed prominently in the ritual area. The participants gather quietly at the ritual site while the celebrant waits elsewhere, out of sight of the ritual area. When it is time for the rite to begin, the celebrant is blindfolded and led into the ritual area by the Assistant. He stands in the center while the ritual begins.

The Ritual
The Assistant quietly marks the ritual space around the entire group of people.

Appearance of the God
The Assistant calls to the god: *Mighty Minotauros, strongest of the strong, born from the union of two worlds, I call on you today to witness the coming into manhood of (_____). Today he stands between the world of childhood and the world of men. Great Minotauros, the strength of your body, your mind and your manhood are renowned among men. Come, bring these strengths to (_____) today as he proves*

himself a man. Join us in this rite.

HP speaks his entrance: *I am here.*

Acknowledgment of the Elements

HP: *We gather together in the sacred circle to celebrate the time of new manhood for (____). This is a time of new beginnings for him, of entrance into the world of man. To acknowledge his growth into manhood and toward maturity, I will introduce him anew to the elements.*

The HP takes the celebrant by the shoulders and guides him to each direction as he acknowledges the elements.

The HP says to the north: *Mighty earth of the north, lusty Faun of the rocks and mountains, I call you to witness the coming into manhood of (____) today. Bring him your steadiness and strength. Welcome.*

The HP says to the east: *Blazing fire of the east, flaming Griffin, I call you to witness the coming into manhood of (____) today. Bring him your vigor and passion. Welcome.*

The HP says to the east: *Rushing water of the east, Naiad of the crashing waves, I call you to witness the coming into manhood of (____) today. Bring him your depth and power. Welcome.*

The HP says to the south: *Blowing winds of the south, ancient and stealthy Sphinx, I call you to witness the coming into manhood of (____) today. Bring him your motion and swiftness. Welcome.*

The HP says to the west: *Ancient ones of the west, wise men who have gone before us, I call you to witness the coming into manhood of (____) today. Bring him your wisdom and vision. Welcome.*

The Initiation

The HP leads the celebrant around the circle, preferably in a 'confused' path, so that all the participants can introduce themselves. The celebrant remains blindfolded as each participant speaks his name to the young man.

When this is finished, the participants begin to clap and chant rhythmically as the HP leads the young man on a walk of disorientation. The HP leads him three times sunwise around the circle, brings him back to the center, and has him turn around in place three times sunwise. Then the HP leads the celebrant over to the trunk or table and has him climb up onto it (still blindfolded) and stand up on it. While he does this, all the participants gather in front of him. Once the celebrant is standing, the HP speaks.

HP: *This sacred space contains the community of men in your life. We have watched you grow from a boy into a young man. You came into this ritual today to show us that you have become a man, that you deserve the respect and the privileges accorded to men. Now we ask that you show us your manly courage. Step forward, find the edge of the (trunk, table, etc.) and jump. You must trust that we will catch you before you come to harm.*

The participants arrange themselves in front of the celebrant so that they can safely catch him when he jumps. When they catch him, they take off his blindfold, cheer him loudly and parade him around the circle on their shoulders.

At this point the HP may present the young man with the privilege he has earned in his new manhood. If the celebrant undertook a hunting or camping trip prior to the ritual, he may display his kill or tell the men about his experiences. This is also the time for a frank discussion of sexuality and the responsibilities that go with it, the celebrant being allowed to ask whatever questions he desires. At this time the young man may also announce a new ritual name.

When the conversation has ended, it is time to bring the rite to an end. The HP acknowledges the celebrant's new social status:

HP: *(_____), you have shown us your courage and your strength. You have grown before our eyes from a boy into a man. We acknowledge you as a man and welcome you to the community of men. Bear your manhood with honor. Carry yourself always so that you will be a source of pride for your family and your community.*

The men may cheer the celebrant one more time.

Farewell to the Elements

The HP bids farewell to the elements.

The HP says to the north: *Weighty earth of the north, lusty Faun of the rocks and mountains, full of steadiness and strength, we thank you for bearing witness to the manhood of (_____). We bid you now return to your dwelling place, with our gratitude. Farewell.*

The HP says to the east: *Blazing fire of the east, flaming Griffin, full of vigor and passion, we thank you for bearing witness to the manhood of (_____). We bid you now return to your dwelling place, with our gratitude. Farewell.*

The HP says to the east: *Rushing water of the east, Naiad of the crashing waves, full of depth and power, we thank you for bearing witness to the manhood of (_____). We bid you now return to your dwelling place, with our gratitude. Farewell.*

The HP says to the south: *Blowing winds of the south, ancient and stealthy Sphinx, full of motion and swiftness, we thank you for bearing witness to the manhood of (_____). We bid you now return to your dwelling place, with our gratitude. Farewell.*

The HP says to the west: *Ancient ones of the west, wise men who have gone before us, we thank you for bearing witness to the manhood of (_____). We bid you now return to your dwelling place, with our gratitude. Farewell.*

Farewell to the God

The Assistant bids farewell to the god: *Mighty Minotauros, strong, virile and wise, we thank you for your presence in our rite, for bearing witness as (_____) took the step from boy to man. Be with him always; share with him your wisdom and strength. Now we bid you return to your dwelling place, with our gratitude. Farewell.*

The HP steps out of view. The Assistant returns the ritual space to the mundane world. The whole gathering may now return joyously to a party in the celebrant's honor. The rite is ended but the journey is just begun.

Initiation

One of **Aphrodite's** pre-Hellenic titles was Fate (**Arachne**) or **Ariadne**, weaver of the threads of life. Ariadne's thread leading **Theseus** out of the labyrinth is the ritual death and rebirth journey guided by the goddess. The cord is the umbilicus, linking humans to the womb-center of being.

The labyrinth which Daedalus built is not a maze. It has only one path which winds like a spiral toward the center. The labyrinth was used for death/rebirth rituals. The **Minotauros** guarded the central underground chamber, symbolic of the underworld and womb. Anyone wishing to learn the secret of the labyrinth, that is, wishing to be 'born again,' had to fight past the bull-monster of their own fears and misconceptions in order to release self and become one with the center.

This initiation ceremony is based on the reconstructed rites which took place on Crete before the coming of the mainland Greeks. In these rituals, the labyrinth was not a physical one, but rather a maze of the mind and the psyche. The labyrinth form represented on the floors of the Minoan temples was used for the Crane Dance. This dance induced a meditative or trance state in the dancer and was a ritual itself. Rather than a complicated dance, however, I have chosen to use an actual labyrinth which the postulant (the person seeking initiation) must enter. The physical act of moving through the spiral path echoes the psychic and emotional journey which the postulant experiences during the ritual.

In this ritual, the postulant must perform all the deliberate actions him/herself. Of course, he or she would first have asked for initiation; whether this request is made of human beings or directly to the gods will depend on each person's tradition and individual inclination. But during the ritual the postulant must also enter the ritual space, call to the goddess, ask to die and be reborn, and find his/her own way into and out of the labyrinth.

This is not a ceremony that involves an officiant initiating someone; it is a ritual in which the postulant steps into the initiation him or herself. The officiants are there simply as guides.

This ritual takes place indoors, in a room which can be closed up or shaded so that it becomes pitch dark. A simple labyrinth is constructed of chairs (with their backs toward the path the postulant will take) or other pieces of furniture draped in sheets. It spirals moonwise from its entrance inward to the center. It needs to have at least one full circuit, but may have more if space permits. Make sure the path within the labyrinth is easy to detect in the dark; place the chairs or other objects close together. You may drape sheets or blankets over the chair backs to simulate a solid wall. You should also cover the entire labyrinth in sheets or blankets so that anyone entering it has to crawl to get through. The space at the very center of the labyrinth should have a folded blanket or a pillow or two for the postulant to sit on.

The altar is set up next to the labyrinth entrance, but out of the way so that it will not be accidentally knocked over. A large labrys stands next to the altar, representing the transformation and rebirth which the postulant will experience during the initiation as well as the balance of energies they seek in life. The ritual space is marked around the entire setup.

The appropriate attire for an initiation is mother-naked, the way we are all born into this world, for initiation is itself a birth. If those involved are uncomfortable with nudity, the postulant should wear simple clothing that will not impede crawling through the labyrinth. There are no 'audience' participants, just the postulant, HPS and Assistant. The HPS wears either metallic clothing or body makeup so that she looks golden. She has a ball of golden thread or yarn long enough to reach all the way through the labyrinth. The Assistant wears a simple tunic or robe.

The postulant waits outside the ritual area, perhaps in the next room. The door to the ritual room is closed or draped so that the postulant cannot see in. The ritual area is lit by one small oil lamp or candle near the doorway, which the Assistant snuffs once the postulant has entered, and one small lamp or candle on the altar, which is lit before the ritual begins. The Assistant has a drum by the altar.

The Ritual

While the postulant waits outside and HPS is hidden within the entrance to the labyrinth, the Assistant marks the ritual space.

The Assistant says:

Between the worlds I take us now
From time and space and mind
A journey safe in goddess' womb
Till out we once more climb

When the Assistant has finished, he calls out in such a way that the postulant can hear him.

Assistant: *The space is made ready for ritual!*

The postulant comes up to the doorway and knocks.

Postulant: *I ask for entrance. I am (_____), child of the gods. I ask to return to the womb of the Great Mother, that I may be reborn with fresh eyes and an open heart into this life.*

The Assistant opens the physical door or pulls aside the drapery, and speaks.

Assistant: *If you wish to enter the sacred space, you must make your own way in.*

The postulant must then open his or her own doorway in the ritual space, walk in, and close the doorway again. The postulant approaches the Assistant (who is standing by the altar) and speaks.

Postulant: *I have entered the sacred space, the womb of the Great Mother, of my own free will and desire. I ask to enter the sacred labyrinth, where I might journey beyond myself and lose myself in the death of initiation. Only then can I be reborn.*

The Assistant answers: *If you wish to enter the sacred labyrinth,* *then you must call upon Ariadne, for only she can guide you where you wish to go.*

Appearance of the Goddess
The postulant calls to the goddess:

Ariadne, young and new,
Come to me alone.
Bring your thread of silken fate
That I may now be shown.

The HPS appears holding the ball of thread and stands next to the altar.

The Initiation
The HPS speaks to the postulant: *You have called me and I have come, carrying in my hands the thread of your life. Ask now what you wish of me.*

The postulant answers: *I desire entrance into the labyrinth, that I may learn the mysteries of life in the hands of the gods.*

Ariadne replies: *If you wish to enter the labyrinth, you must give yourself up to me. Take this thread; it is your connection to the Great Mother. You must find your own way through the labyrinth. The thread of your fate leads ever to me; unwind the ball as you go so that you may find your way back to the outer world once the journey is ended.*

Now begin the journey to the depths. Move through the labyrinth until you can go no further. When you have reached the end, call to me.

The HPS hands the ball of thread to the postulant and motions him/her to enter the labyrinth. When the postulant enters the labyrinth, the Assistant extinguishes the lamp or candle which is on the altar so the room is pitch dark. The postulant will have to feel his/her way through the labyrinth. The Assistant drums a slow heartbeat while the postulant moves through the labyrinth. When the postulant calls out that he/she has reached the end, the Assistant stops drumming. All remains totally quiet for three to four minutes. Finally, Ariadne speaks.

Ariadne: *You have reached the center of the labyrinth and you are nothing. You have accomplished the loss of everything that is you. You have no sight, no will, no name. You float in the darkness of the womb of the Great Mother, connected only to me by the golden thread. I am all your fate, all your will. The sound of my voice is your universe.*

You are completely helpless but completely safe. And, though you are by yourself, you are not alone. Here, then, is the mystery: the golden thread is within you always, connecting you to the source of life itself. When you are born into this life you bring with you a spark of the gods, a taste of the divine source whence you came. See this within you now, the eternal flame of the gods which stretches into a golden thread and reaches out from you to connect you with all creation. No matter what your will or your desire, you cannot break this thread or extinguish this flame.

The secret is in the remembering, for though we know at birth that we are all a part of the Great Mother, the trials of this life wipe the memory from our minds. But in our hearts we still remember. Feel the spark within you and remember that divine place from which you have come.

[Pause.]

As you were born into this world from your mother's body and from the Great Mother, so now will you be reborn to this world. As with your first birth, you enter the world again of your own will. Follow the thread of your fate and find your way out of the labyrinth. I await your arrival.

The HPS waits by the entrance to the labyrinth. The Assistant stands by the altar. When the postulant is near the entrance to the labyrinth, the Assistant lights the lamp or candle on the altar again. When the postulant comes out of the entrance, the HPS and Assistant hug him/her and welcome him/her into the world.

The HPS speaks the words of welcome: *Welcome again to the world of the living. With love and trust you have made a difficult journey into the labyrinth and into yourself. I honor your courage and the divine within you.*

The HPS gives the postulant a blessing, using whichever gesture she prefers. Then the Assistant speaks.

Assistant: *Remember this well: where you have journeyed, now you know the way. You have found once again your connection with the divine, the spark within you that makes you a child of the gods. Make this knowledge a part of your life. And should you ever need to return to the labyrinth, all you need do is look within you. You know the way.*

The HPS presents the postulant with the ball of golden thread. The postulant will keep this thread as a ritual item representing this initiation.

Farewell to the Goddess

The postulant must now bid farewell to Ariadne. As he/she finishes the devocation, the HPS disappears into the labyrinth.

The postulant says:

Ariadne, bright and fair,
All honor to your name.
I thank you for your presence here
And bid you return whence you came.

The Assistant returns the ritual space to the mundane world, saying:

Take down the walls and open the door
From edgeless space and endless time
The sacred space shall be no more
From goddess' womb we now do climb.

The rite is ended.

Rite of Betrothal

Another of **Aphrodite**'s names is **Ariadne**, meaning 'Very Holy One.' She is an aspect of the Minoan Great Goddess whom the Hellenes later recast as a human maiden. In her guise as Ariadne she was also called **Alpheta**, *alpha* and *eta* being the first and last letters of her name. As Alpheta she was guardian of the Corona Borealis (Crown of the North Wind) whence her consort and sweet lover **Hermes** conducted souls. She lived in a silver-circled castle much like the Welsh Caer Arianrhod.

Hermes is a pre-Hellenic god, though the name we know him by comes to us from the Greeks. He was one of the Aegean great mother's primal serpent-consorts, partaking of her wisdom because he was once a part of her. In early times his caduceus was topped with a solar/lunar disk bearing horns in the shape of snakes' heads. Hermes' efficacy in both healing and conducting souls depended on his union with Aphrodite for completion, for they were truly two halves of a greater whole. The two made into one became **Ouroboros**, the great serpent which encircles and embodies all of creation. The two serpents on Hermes' caduceus represent the intertwining of the two halves which make the whole, much as the Hindus represent the two halves of the body's energy by two serpents called Kundalini and Shakti.

Hermes is associated with **Asclepius**, who may simply have been another Greek name for him. Asclepius also carried a double-serpent caduceus. Asclepius and Hermes share the ability to perform magical healings on those who come to them for aid. The cock was sacred to Asclepius as the god who could resurrect the dead, just as the rooster heralds the birth of the day. In this aspect Asclepius was also connected with the image of the phallus through the process of dying and rising again, thus a symbol of virility and libido.

At Knossos the people ritually re-enacted the mating of the primal couple under a sycamore fig (*Ficus sycamorus*) tree. This ritual was an early version of the *hieros gamos,* or sacred marriage, which united humankind with the divine. The Greeks later renamed this tale as the mating of Zeus and **Rhea**/Hera or Zeus and **Europa**, though the Minoans apparently did not use these same names for the divine couple. Should the couple to be betrothed be of the same gender, they may choose to substitute matching deities from the list in Part One, or they may consider Ariadne and Hermes as symbolic of energies rather than physical bodies.

This ritual is designed to be held at dawn or very early in the morning, preferably outside where the sun can be seen to rise over the horizon. The beginning of the day is a symbolic time, appropriate for a ritual which expresses a beginning for two people.

The two who wish to express their intent to wed each bring with them into the ceremony area a blade (knife, which must be sharp), which is a symbol of their will, and an item of great personal (sentimental, not monetary) value. The couple may hold these items until they are needed or they may place them on the altar as the ritual begins. The altar contains, in addition to any tools or symbolic objects the couple would like, a piece of cord about two meters long, thin enough to be cut easily by the blades the couple bring.

The ritual involves only one officiant, since the couple perform the ceremony themselves with the officiant simply presiding. There may also be a priestess and priest present who embody the deities invoked. They should remain hidden until the deities are called upon, at which time they step into view.

The Ritual

The couple declaring their intent are seated on the ground in the center of the ritual area, as close together as they can comfortably sit. The participants are gathered around them.

The officiant marks the sacred space around the group, saying:
I draw the shape of endless time,
A circle cut from edgeless space.
From out the center now do climb
These two who shall stand face to face.

Acknowledgment of the Elements

The couple acknowledge the elements, dividing them however they choose.

The couple say to the north: *Wide earth, mother's body, foundation of all, come now and witness our joyous rite. Anchor us all in your ancient love. Make steadfast and constant those gathered here in celebration of love.*

The couple say to the east: *Fire of dawn, light of day, spark of love, come now and witness our joyous rite. Spread your warmth across the land as our love and passion grow. Light now the faces of those gathered here in celebration of love.*

The couple say to the east: *Deep waters, womb of life, vessel of faith, come now and witness our joyous rite. Stir from your depths the wisdom of the infinite, that we may taste the mystery of the unknowable. Surround and fill the hearts of those gathered here in celebration of love.*

The couple say to the south: *Gentle wind, breath of the divine, blowing spirit, come now and witness our joyous rite. Brush gently across us all that you may awaken us to greater life and greater love. Breathe sweetly on those gathered here in celebration of love.*

The couple say to the west: *Ancient ones, ancestors on whose shoulders we stand, come now and witness our joyous rite. Stir within us the memory of the thread that connects us all. Surround and embrace those gathered here in celebration of love.*

Appearance of the Deities

The officiant calls to the goddess and god:

Ariadne, sweet and fair,
Come to us on morning air.
Bring your thread of silken fate
As you rise to meet your mate.
Come now Hermes, swift and sure,
Bringing movement, light and pure.
Rise up, rise up with morning's sun
To meet your love, to become one.

If a priestess and priest are participating, personifying the deities, they should step into view now.

The Betrothal

The officiant: *As the god and goddess are but two halves of one greater whole, incomplete each without the other, so do humans long for the completion of their other half. But, imperfect as we are, our judgments come hard in these matters. These two you see before you have chosen one another to keep company. Today they choose to take a further step, to make public their intent to build a permanent bond. May you be witness to their actions.*

The officiant steps out of the way and the couple step to the center, in front of the altar. Each in turn holds up his or her ritual blade to show it to the participants, and speaks.

Couple: *This blade is a solid object which symbolizes an abstract concept. Today may my will be as solid as this (steel, iron, etc.) and as sharp in intent as its edge.*

The two then together pick up the length of cord from the altar. Each measures out a piece of cord the length of their arm from the elbow to the end of the middle finger, then cuts the cord to that length. Each then shows the cord to those present. They present the cords to each other, and speak.

Couple: *With this cord I take my measure, a piece of who I am. I offer it to you in safekeeping as we two begin our journey together. Keep it safe for me until the time comes when I offer to bind myself to you with it.*

Each then shows the participants the items they have brought into circle. They offer the items to each other, and speak.

Couple: *This [item] touches a place in my heart, as you touch a place in my heart. I treasure this [item] for it means much to me. I offer it to you in token of my trust for you. Keep it safe for me until the time we become as one. Then it shall belong not to one, but to us both together.*

Farewell to the Deities

The couple kiss as public acknowledgment of their affection. The officiant faces the couple speaks.

Officiant: *Those present have heard your intent. May the sun and moon, the wind and the water bear witness to your love. May all the gods bless your journey together. Step gently on your path.*

As Ariadne and Hermes are but two halves of a whole, so are we all parts of a greater one. Blessed Lord and Lady, lover and beloved, we thank you for your presence this day, your witness to this rite. Grant that your example may lie close to the hearts of these two. Return now to your dwelling place with our gratitude and love.

If a priestess and priest have personified the deities during the ritual, they now step out of sight until the ritual is over.

Farewell to the Elements

The officiant bids farewell to the elements and closes the ritual.

Officiant: *Burning fire, rushing water, blowing wind, settling earth, blessed ancestors: you bear witness this day to a remarkable act, a choice of the heart. We thank you for your presence, the blessing of your being upon these two. Return now to your dwelling place with our thanks.*

And as these two, so may we all be: smaller parts of the greater whole. And as the great circle of all existence, may their union continue into eternity.

The participants hold hands in a circle around the couple as the officiant returns the ritual space to the mundane world.

The time after the betrothal should be spent working together under the guidance of a spiritual teacher to decide if permanent union is the right choice for the couple. Should they choose not to wed, each may formally request their cord and token be returned. Should they choose to wed, the cord and token are used in the marriage ceremony which follows.

Ceremony of Marriage

The ceremony takes place well before noon, though not necessarily at dawn. It can be performed alone but is designed as the second half of a set of rituals, the Rite of Betrothal being the first half. The ceremony is performed by the couple, with a Priestess and Priest officiating, aided by the Assistant.

The ritual area is prepared as usual, with the addition of the following: the two cords and the two token items used in the betrothal ceremony are placed prominently on the altar. There is also a third cord, about the same length as the other two but of a different color or material. Should the couple be of the same gender, they may choose to substitute matching deities from the list in Part One, or they may consider Ariadne and Hermes as symbolic of energies rather than physical bodies. The wedding feast is set apart from the ritual area but nearby enough that the couple can easily be carried to the site by the participants. The wedding begins as did the betrothal.

The Ritual

The couple to wed are seated on the ground in the center of the ritual area, as close together as they can comfortably be. The participants are gathered around them.

The Assistant marks the sacred space around the group, saying:

I draw the shape of endless time,
A circle cut from edgeless space.
From out the center now do climb
These two who shall stand face to face.

Appearance of the Deities

The Assistant calls to the goddess:

Ariadne, sweet and fair,
Come to us on morning air.

Bring your thread of silken fate
As you rise to meet your mate.
The HPS steps into view and speaks.
HPS: *I am here.*
The Assistant calls to the god:
Come now Hermes, swift and sure,
Bringing movement, light and pure.
Rise up, rise up with morning's sun
To meet your love, to become one.
The HP steps into view and speaks.
HP: *I am here.*

Acknowledgment of the Elements

The HPS and HP acknowledge the elements.

The HP/HPS say to the north: *Wide earth, mother's body, foundation of all, come now and witness this our joyous rite. Anchor these two, anchor us all in the beat of your ancient heart. Make steadfast and constant those gathered here in celebration of love.*

The HP/HPS say to the east: *Fire of dawn, light of day, spark of love, come now and witness this our joyous rite. Spread your warmth across the land as the love and passion between these two grows. Light now the faces of those gathered here in celebration of love.*

The HP/HPS say to the east: *Deep waters, womb of life, vessel of faith, come now and witness this our joyous rite. Stir from your depths the wisdom of the infinite, that we may taste the mystery of belief in the unknowable. Surround and fill the hearts of those gathered here in celebration of love.*

The HP/HPS say to the south: *Gentle wind, breath of the gods, blowing spirit, come now and witness this our joyous rite. Brush gently across these two that you may awaken them to greater life, greater love. Breathe sweetly on those gathered here in celebration of love.*

The HP/HPS say to the west: *Ancient ones, ancestors on whose shoulders we stand, come now and witness this our joyous rite. Stir within us the memory of the thread that connects us all. Surround and* *embrace those gathered here in celebration of love.*

The Marriage

HPS and HP begin the rite with the following exchange:

HP: *As the god and goddess are but two halves of one greater whole,*

HPS: *Incomplete each without the other,*

HP: *So do humans long for the completion of their other half.*

HPS: *As Hermes to Ariadne, as sun to moon, night to day,*

HP: *Now are [names of couple] come together before us.*

The couple step to the altar and pick up the token objects and cords used in the rite of betrothal. Each holds up the object and cord which the other gave to them during the betrothal ceremony.

Each one says: *This cord is a measure of the one I choose for my lifemate, given to me in love. This [object] is a token of [his/her] trust in me that I may keep safe something [he/she] holds dear. This cord now becomes a symbol of the bond between us, and the [object] becomes ours together as we join to become one.*

The HPS holds the third cord for all to see and speaks.

HPS: *Each of these two is an individual, a spark of life within the cosmos. But when they join together they create a third spark, that which is their union. As each of these cords* [gesturing to the cords the couple are holding] *represents the heart of its owner, so does this third cord represent the heart of their marriage, created from the love between them.*

I am Ariadne, Weaver of the Web of Life. I know the magic of threads and knots, and I know the magic of love in one's heart. You two who love each other, whose hearts are joined together, join your two cords together now with this third one. Complete the cord, complete the magic.

The couple hold the three cords for all to see as they braid them together into a single rope. The HPS and HP bind the couple's wrists together with the braid.

The couple speak the following vows to each other: *As our* *wrists are bound by this cord, let our lives be bound by the same fate, let our paths run side by side and our hearts hold fast together. For the rest of this life I choose you above all others, to love and support, to trust, to keep safe, to help grow. By the Lady of Love and her beloved Lord I swear these things to you.*

The couple raise their hands together, showing their wrists bound together.

HP: *What is sworn before the gods, let all mortals hold dear.*

If the couple have chosen to exchange rings, they do so now. Each should hold up the ring they will put on the other's finger, and look at the other through the hole in the ring before putting it on their partner's finger.

The HPS directs the participants to turn towards the rising sun, towards the east, and speaks.

HPS: *As the sun rises and the light of day grows, so may your love grow to light the hearts of all alive. May the sun and moon, the wind and the water bear witness to your love.*

The couple may now kiss as a token of the bond they are sealing.

Farewell to the Elements

The couple stand in the center of the sacred space, with participants around the edge, as the HPS and HP bid farewell to the elements.

HP: *Burning fire, rushing water, blowing wind, settling earth, blessed ancestors: you bear witness this day to a remarkable act, a choice of heart, a bonding of souls. We thank you for your presence, the blessing of your being upon these two. Depart now whence you came with our thanks.*

HPS: *And as these two, and as the Lady and her beloved Lord, so may we all be: fundamental parts of the greater whole. And as the circle, may their union continue into eternity.*

Farewell to the Deities

The Assistant bids farewell to the deities and closes the ritual.

Assistant: *As Ariadne and Hermes are but two halves of a whole, so are we all parts of a greater one.*

Sweet Lord, beloved Hermes, we thank you for your blessing of light, of love, of completion of the whole. Grant that your example may lie close to the hearts of these two who also love. Join us now in the celebration of the union of these two, for all marriages are a celebration of you as well. When the feasting has ended we ask that you return to your dwelling place with our gratitude and love.

The HP steps out of view.

Assistant: *Lady of Love, sweet Ariadne, we thank you for your blessing of passion, of connection, of strength in gentleness. Grant that your example may lie close to the hearts of these two who also love. Join us now in the celebration of the union of these two, for all marriages are a celebration of you as well. When the feasting has ended we ask that you return to your dwelling place with our gratitude and love.*

The HPS steps out of view.

The participants join hands to encircle the newly wedded couple.

The Assistant opens the sacred space, then declares:

May the deities be praised!

May the feast be set!

May the celebration begin!

The couple are carried out of the circle on the shoulders of their friends and family and processed loudly and with great merrymaking to the feast area. They should be given the seat of honor at the feast, for today they are indeed the Lady and her Lord. They may remove the cord from around their wrists once they have left the ritual area. They should store it carefully and with respect, because it represents each of them and the relationship they have now formalized.

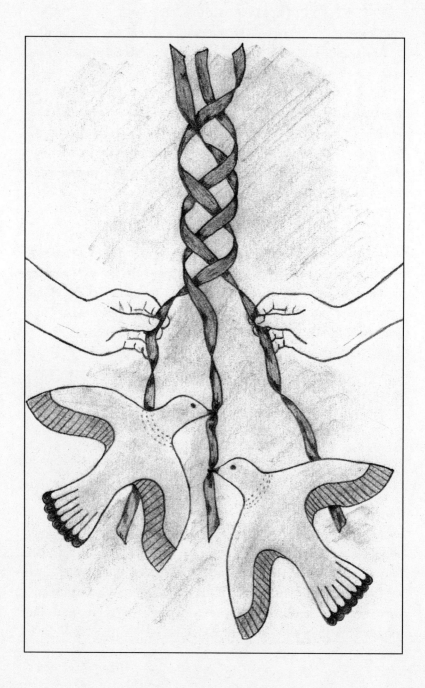

Rite of Parting

Though often a sad or unpleasant situation, the occasion of parting is sometimes a necessary one as we move and grow through life. When the parting is that of a married couple or of very close friends, this rite can be used to acknowledge the separating of ways as a necessary act and put a formal closure on the relationship. The deities used for this ritual are **Ariadne** and **Rhea**, Ariadne as the spinner and subsequent cutter of the threads of our life paths, and Rhea as the Great Mother to whom everything must return. The strong female energy of two Priestesses rather than a Priestess/Priest couple emphasizes the healing feminine principle within us all. This energy is directed toward the goal of allowing the couple to part ways gently and heal themselves as they go.

If the two to be parted did not make a triple braid (as in the marriage ceremony above) in a previous ritual, they should make one before the rite of parting. Each person has a single cord which represents him/her. There is also a third cord which represents the relationship. The two making the braid should put the energy and feelings of the relationship into the third cord as they add it into the braid. The three cords need to be distinct and recognizable; it is best if they are three different colors or textures. The braid should be knotted at both ends. It is placed on the altar prior to the ritual.

The ritual can be adapted for the parting of a group or three or four people. Simply add more cords to the braid and have each participant repeat the words the couple speaks in the ritual. There should still be only one cord to represent the soul of the relationship.

This ritual is performed outdoors if possible; the time of day is not important. An appropriate date for this ritual is the new moon, a time of new beginnings and of leaving behind the old.

Two Priestesses and an Assistant preside. One Priestess embodies Ariadne and another Rhea, but the two who are parting actually perform the ceremony themselves.

The Ariadne Priestess needs to have a very sharp knife, preferably her ritual knife. There is a hole dug in the ground in front of the altar before the ritual begins.

The Ritual

The couple to be parted stand in the center of the ritual area, with the participants gathered around them. The two Priestesses are hidden within the ritual area.

The Assistant marks the ritual space around the group, saying:

Between the worlds I take us now
From time and space and mind
A journey safe in goddess' womb
Till out we once more climb

Appearance of the Deities

The Assistant calls to the goddess as Rhea: *Holy Rhea, great mother of all, we call to you: come to us now. Bring us your ancient wisdom, your strength and compassion, the all-encompassing healing love of the mother. Welcome.*

The Rhea Priestess steps into view and says: *She is here.*

The Assistant calls to the goddess as Ariadne: *Holy Ariadne, spinner of the golden thread of fate, weaver of the web of life, we call to you: come to us now. Bring us your clear vision, the knowledge of the web that binds us each to a life path, whether those paths cross or part. Welcome.*

The Ariadne Priestess steps into view and says: *She is here.*

Acknowledgement of the Elements

The two priestesses divide the elemental invocations between them as desired.

The Priestesses say to the north: *Great earth of the north, body of life, come now and witness this our solemn rite. Bring us your ancient steadfastness, the knowledge of the place whence we all come and whither we all must return. Welcome.*

The Priestesses say to the east: *Bright fire of the east, light of new dawn, come now and witness this our solemn rite. Bring us the brilliant light of the new that wipes away the shadows of the old and lights a new path to follow. Welcome.*

The Priestesses say to the east: *Wide waters of the east, deep sea-womb of life, come now and witness this our solemn rite. Bring us the wisdom of the infinite deep, the unfathomable abyss from which we all rise. Welcome.*

The Priestesses say to the south: *Gentle winds of the south, breath of the divine, come now and witness this our solemn rite. Bring us the gentle, sure breeze that cleanses the path it touches to make way for the new. Welcome.*

The Priestesses say to the west: *Blessed ancestors of the west, those on whose shoulders we stand, come now and witness this our solemn rite. Bring us the remembrance of who we are, whether we walk together or separately. Welcome.*

The Parting

The two Priestesses motion those to be parted to move to the altar. The couple stand between the Priestesses. The couple pick up the braid and show it to everyone present. They speak together.

Both: *This braid represents the intertwining of our life paths.*

One: *There is a cord within the braid which represents my individual path.*

Other: *There is a cord within the braid which represents my individual path.*

Both: *Twined together with the soul of our relationship.*

Each one speaks the following: *As the paths of our lives once grew together, now they have grown apart. I call on Ariadne, spinner of the thread, weaver of the web, to help me separate my path from*

187

yours, that we may each follow where we need to go. I ask this in under-standing and in peace.

The couple hold the braid together. The Ariadne Priestess steps up to them and cuts the knots off the ends of the braids with her knife. Then she speaks.

Ariadne Priestess: *The knots are severed, the ties broken. You may each take the thread of your own path to follow as your life dictates. But remember, there is also the soul of your relationship.*

The couple separate out their individual threads and put them away (in a pocket or pouch). They hold up the remaining thread, the one which symbolizes the soul of their relationship.

Each of the couple says: *Mother Rhea, I call on you now and ask this of you: our paths have grown apart and it is time for the energy which we put into the relationship to return whence it came. Accept it back into the earth, that it may again become a part of the greater whole. I ask this in understanding and in peace.*

The Rhea Priestess steps forward and takes the remaining cord. She places it in the hole which has been dug in front of the altar and covers it over with earth. Then she speaks.

Rhea Priestess: *What has come from the mother returns to the mother. All things pass in their own time. Grieve for what is gone but know that all life moves as it must.*

A brief silence is observed in honor of the choice the couple have made.

Farewell to the Elements

The Priestesses bid farewell to the elements, dividing the directions between them as desired.

The Priestesses say to the north: *Great earth of the north, body of life, we thank you for your presence in this our solemn rite, for your ancient steadfastness, the knowledge of the place whence we all come and whither we all must return. We bid you now return to your dwelling place. Farewell.*

The Priestesses say to the east: *Bright fire of the east, light of* *new dawn, we thank you for your presence in this our solemn rite, for the brilliant light of the new that wipes away the shadows of the old and lights a new path to follow. We bid you now return to your dwelling place. Farewell.*

The Priestesses say to the east: *Wide waters of the east, deep sea-womb of life, we thank you for your presence in this our solemn rite, for the wisdom of the infinite deep, the unfathomable abyss from which we all rise. We bid you now return to your dwelling place. Farewell.*

The Priestesses say to the south: *Gentle winds of the south, breath of the divine, we thank you for your presence in this our solemn rite, for the gentle, sure breeze that cleanses the path it touches to make way for the new. We bid you now return to your dwelling place. Farewell.*

The Priestesses say to the west: *Blessed ancestors of the west, those on whose shoulders we stand, we thank you for your presence in this our solemn rite, for the remembrance of who we are, whether we walk together or separately. We bid you now return to your dwelling place. Farewell.*

Farewell to the Deities

The Assistant bids farewell to the goddess as Ariadne: *Holy Ariadne, spinner of the thread of fate, weaver of the web of life, we thank you for your presence in our rite. Farewell.*

The Ariadne Priestess steps out of view.

The Assistant bids farewell to the goddess as Rhea: *Holy Rhea, great mother of all, we thank you for your presence in our rite. Farewell.*

The Rhea Priestess steps out of view.

The Assistant returns the ritual space to the mundane world:

Take down the walls and open the door
From edgeless space and endless time
The sacred space shall be no more
From goddess' womb we now do climb.

The rite is ended.

Memorial Rite

The earliest evidence we have of religion in human culture is the remains of various burials. From the simplest image of an ancient body buried in the fetal position to the elaborate funeral settings of Egypt, Native America and Crete we see a constant: humankind's concern with the afterlife. Whether the body is carefully preserved or returned to the earth or sea, the memorial rite formalizes, for those still living, the end of one phase of existence and the beginning of the next. Such rituals serve not so much to aid the deceased as to comfort those who remain after and to remind us that we are all part of the great wheel of life, ever turning, never ending.

Like modern neo-pagans, the Minoans believed in the cycle of birth, death and rebirth. Their mother-goddess **Rhea** accepts back in death those to whom she has given life. And she keeps them safe until it is time for them to return again to this world. While Rhea is the steady, constant heartbeat of the great mother, her consort **Cronos** represents the motion of the cycles. In his being we find the movement from birth through growth and eventually to death and rebirth. As Father Time, he presides over the ever-shifting cycles of life while Rhea as Mother Time is the great womb from which everything is born and to which everything must return.

This Memorial Rite may be used either as a funeral rite or as a memorial ceremony separate from the funeral. The altar should be decorated to represent the departed, with mementos from his or her life and perhaps photographs as well. There should be a small oil lamp in the center of the altar. The labrys, prominently displayed, represents transformation and regeneration, and reminds the participants of the ever-turning wheel of birth, death and rebirth.

Those attending the rite may bring with them small objects

which represent their relationship with the departed. Dress need not be somber, for though the occasion may be sad, it is also a celebration of the great wheel of life which contains both light and dark.

A custom common on Crete for a number of centuries was the drinking of toasts to departed friends and family. A man or woman would take a cup of wine or other drink to the tomb of a loved one and drink to their life and their spirit. When the cup was drained, the person would throw it at the tomb and smash it, showing that it was empty and that they had drunk the whole cup in honor of the departed. For this ritual, have ready some wine or other beverage and an expendable goblet in which to share it. Be sure that the goblet is made of ceramic or some other breakable material, but preferably not glass, as its shattering could be quite dangerous. Metal, while attractive, will not have the same effect during the ritual.

The participants gather in the ritual area before the ceremony begins. The HP and HPS should be people who were close to the departed, perhaps family members or good friends. They are hidden out of sight as the Assistant begins.

The Ritual

The participants are gathered in the ritual area; the Assistant marks the sacred space around them.

The Assistant says:

We cast the sacred space all round,
Above, below and through the earth;
The ancient womb created now,
The place of birth and death and birth.

Appearance of the Deities

The Assistant calls to the goddess:

Mother Rhea, Womb of Matter, from whom everything comes and to whom everything must return in its time, we call you: come to us now.

Bring us your compassion, your ancient wisdom, the knowledge and faith of the great mother. Welcome.

The HPS steps into view and says: *She is here.*

The Assistant calls to the god: *Cronos, Father Time, keeper of the cycle that turns the wheel of life, we call to you: come to us now. Bring us your compassion, your ancient wisdom, the knowledge and faith of the ageless father. Welcome.*

The HP steps into view and says: *He is here.*

The Memorial

HP and HPS turn to face the participants.

HPS: *There is an anchor in the life we experience, the source of the life we experience: the great mother, manifested to us as the earth herself. She gives us life and sustains our life and when the time comes, she accepts us back to her as a mother gathering her children to her heart.*

One among us has taken a step the rest of us have not yet experienced. (_____) has left the life of the physical body and returned to the source, to the place from which all life comes. We are gathered here together to celebrate the life of (_____) and to remember (him/her) and our experiences together.

The HPS lights the lamp in the center of the altar.

HPS: *The flame of (his/her) life still burns bright before us in our hearts and minds. So may it always be.*

We have brought with us tangible parts of our lives with (_____), items that connect us with (him/her). Let each of us share with the others how (_____) has touched us. Let us share in (his/her) honor.

HP and HPS may go first to put the others at ease. Each person who wishes to participate may show the memento he or she has brought and tell about his or her experiences with the departed. The participants may place their items on the altar if they wish. When all who wish to do so have shared their thoughts, the HP speaks.

HP: *I am the sower and the seed, the reaper and the harvest. Each of us is a part of the great cycle: in the field the seed sprouts, grows, ripens, and falls, to nourish the earth for the next season when the fields will grow green again. Though we can only see a small part of the great cycle, we can feel its power and know its wholeness. We know that we are all a part of this great wondrous whole, that each of us moves through the sacred cycles as we experience life.*

And though we cannot see where (_____) has gone, we cannot see to the next step in the cycle until we reach it ourselves, we know that the wheel turns as it always has and always will. The Ageless Father watches over us as we move through the cycles. The Great Mother holds and protects us from birth to birth.

Let us celebrate the cycles, the life of (_____) and all life in its many forms and stages. We have shared our thoughts with each other. Now let us share a drink, a toast to (_____), in celebration of (his/her) life on this earth.

The HP and HPS fill the goblet with wine.

The HP dedicates the toast: *To (_____)!*

The HP takes a drink, then hands the goblet to the next person around the circle and instructs them to do the same. The goblet is passed around the circle, each person drinking a toast to the departed. When the goblet reaches the HPS, she drinks all that remains and exclaims.

HPS: *We have drained the cup in your honor, (_____)! We bid you all the gods' blessings on your journeys, wherever you may go, until the day when we will meet again.*

The HPS throws the goblet to the ground, breaking it. The participants all exclaim blessings to the departed's name.

Farewell to the Deities

When all is quiet again, the Assistant bids farewell to the deities and ends the ritual.

Assistant: *Mother Rhea, Womb of Matter, from whom everything comes and to whom everything must return in its time, we thank you* *for your presence in our rite, for your compassion, your ancient wisdom, the knowledge and faith of the Great Mother. We bid you now return to your dwelling place, with our gratitude and love. Farewell.*

The HPS steps out of view.

Assistant: *Cronos, Father Time, keeper of the cycle that turns the wheel of life, we thank you for your presence in our rite, for your compassion, your ancient wisdom, the knowledge and faith of the Ageless Father. We bid you now return to your dwelling place, with our gratitude and love. Farewell.*

The HP steps out of view.

The Assistant returns the ritual space to the mundane world:

The life and love, both whole and part,
Remain forever in our hearts;
The space wherein the rite was done
Returns now to the greater one.

The rite is ended. The altar lamp which represents the departed may be left (NEVER UNATTENDED) to burn out. Alternately, it may be extinguished and given to the departed's close family for use as a remembrance on their personal altar.

Ceremony to Honor the Ancestors

One type of ritual which the Minoans enacted regularly is something modern neo-pagans may find unusual: the dining ceremony. It grew out of the oldest religious activity on Crete, the rites centered around the ancestors' burial places. Like the ceremonies performed in front of the tombs on the plain of Messara, the purpose of this ritual is the celebration of those who have died but whose memory (and genes) live on in us. The simplest form of dining ceremony is a communal meal where a place has been set at the table for each ancestor who is to be honored. The ancestors are 'invited to dinner' along with the living members of the family, the meal taken together being a kind of communion (being in community) with the ancestral spirits.

This ritual bears a resemblance to the European Dumb Supper traditionally held at Samhain. Both activities involve a meal of special dishes prepared to honor and 'feed' the spirits of those who have died. The ancient Greeks, as well, prepared special meals to honor and nourish the spirits. Their ceremonies involved the sacrifice of an animal, usually a goat, whose blood they poured out onto the ground for the spirits of the dead. The meat was then roasted and shared among those present in honor of the spirits.

As with many of their traditions, the Minoans developed a formal setting for the dining ritual, constructing special rooms and even whole buildings for these ceremonies. These structures included kitchens or preparation areas as well as dining rooms. The food served at these rituals was purchased and prepared especially for the ritual and was not a part of the regular household food. As such it was separate and sacred, a part of the ritual rather than the everyday household activity.

It is likely that special dishes were served during dining rites, perhaps the favorite foods of those within the family who had died. These dishes would have been reserved for the dining rituals only and not cooked at other times. The choice of foods usually included wine, some of which was offered as a libation to the ancestors, and bread which was specially made for the ritual. The serving ware – cups, bowls, pitchers and so forth – used for dining rituals was also kept separate from the ordinary crockery and used only for ritual purposes.

While we do not have the luxury of specially-built rooms and separate sets of dishes for our dining rituals, we can still create a ceremonial atmosphere using the resources we have available. This ritual can easily take place in your dining room with your usual table and chairs. The Minoans sat on long built-in benches with small movable tables placed in front of them, but modern furniture serves the purpose just as well. In keeping with the sacred nature of the ceremony, take care in choosing serving ware and accessories. Rather than your everyday dishes, get out the ones you save for special occasions. Decorate with platters of fresh fruit and vases of flowers. When setting your table, be sure to include enough dishes for all the ancestors as well as the living guests. If you use a tablecloth, make sure that it is washable; the wine goblets will be repeatedly turned upside down and set on the table. The few drops of wine that remain in each goblet might stain a delicate or light-colored cloth.

If this is to be a family ceremony, you might decide ahead of time which ancestors will be invited and set their places together at one end of the table. However, if a group of friends will partic-ipate in this ceremony, they should each invite one ancestor to the ritual. They may bring a picture or memento of the ancestor to set at the ancestor's place during the meal. If this is to be a gathering of friends, set each ancestor's place next to the guest to whom they are related.

For this rite, decide on your menu ahead of time. Have the dishes prepared before the participants arrive so that you may concentrate on the ritual rather than the kitchen. You might make a mini-ritual out of the food preparation, especially if the dishes were favorites of the ancestors being honored. If there will be very many people involved, you might ask each of them to prepare and bring a dish appropriate to the ancestor they have chosen to honor.

Decide beforehand where each participant will sit. Mark their place at the table with their name on a card or other nameplate, and set a place beside them for the ancestor they will honor during the ritual. Have goblets or wine glasses at each place, including enough for the ancestors. Be sure to set a chair for each ancestor as well. The spirits shouldn't have to stand at a dinner in their honor.

Provide plenty of wine or other beverage for this ceremony. Each ancestor's cup must be filled, and the participants will drink toasts to the ancestor as well. You might offer a choice of beverages – wine, sparkling apple cider, fruit punch – so the participants may select a non-alcoholic beverage if they wish. This is especially important if there will be children present.

This is one ritual in which children may participate fully. They may simply attend the meal or they may each honor an ancestor as well. This is a good setting for the thoughtful remembrance of relatives who have died during the child's lifetime. Even a young child can offer a toast to Great-Grandma and tell everyone about the cookies she used to bake or the stories she used to tell.

The Ritual

The participants gather in the dining area. The table is set with one place for each living participant and one place for each ancestor. The food is arranged on the table, each special dish set next to the place of the ancestor whom it commemorates. There is one officiant, the Host (this may be a man or woman) seated prominently, perhaps at the head of the table. This person directs the activities of the ceremony and ensures that no one is left out. The participants perform the ceremony themselves, of course.

The participants find their places at the table and stand behind their chairs. They may set mementos of the ancestors at the ancestors' places at the table.

The Host begins the ceremony: *We come together to celebrate the lives of those who have gone before us and who live in us still. As we share the food that sustains our bodies, we also share the memories that sustain our souls. Let us honor the Ancestors. Let us invite them to dine with us and share our meal as we celebrate their lives and their legacy.*

Each participant silently invites his or her ancestor to the table. When all have done so, the Host motions for the group to sit. Wine and other beverages are passed around the table. Each participant fills his or her own cup as well as the cup of the ancestor they honor. When all the cups are filled, the Host speaks.

Host: *Today we join in a meal with those who gave us our life and our lineage. We honor their lives, which are our history. Let us drink a toast to them as we celebrate: To the Ancestors!*

The participants all toast: *To the Ancestors!*

They immediately drink from their cups.

The Host then instructs the participants in the method of honoring the ancestors: Beginning with the Host, each person around the table will highlight a specific ancestor. To do this, the participant names the ancestor and their relationship to that person. He or she describes the importance of the ancestor in their life and may share a photograph or other memento, if desired. Then he or she shows everyone the special dish which has been prepared in honor of this ancestor. The participant then serves a portion of this special dish to the ancestor and to him or herself, and passes the dish around the table, each participant taking a portion. Do not forget to serve each ancestor as well. The servings for the ancestors may be token amounts. After all, spirits do not eat that much.

When the dish returns to the participant who shared it, he or she stands and offers a toast in honor of the ancestor. Everyone drinks the toast, but the participant who gives the toast must empty his or her cup. (It might be wise not to fill your cup too full at the beginning of the ceremony if you're having wine.)

The participant then turns the cup upside down on the table and announces to the ancestor: *I have emptied my cup in your honor.*

This ritual continues until each participant has shared food and offered a toast to his or her ancestor. Those who have emptied their cups may refill them to toast the other ancestors if they wish. Once all the ancestors have been toasted and all the food has been shared around the table, it is time for the meal itself to begin. The conversation should center around the ancestors being honored and their impact on the lives of the participants. No one should touch the food or drink offered to the ancestors. After all, you would not take the food off another dinner guest's plate, would you?

When the meal has ended, it is time to end the ritual as well. All the participants stand as the Host proclaims the final toast.

Host: *Noble Ancestors, we honor your spirit in our lives! We thank you for your gracious company at our meal today and bid you sweet blessings in your realm. We empty our cups to you in honor and praise!*

The participants drink what remains in their cups and all turn them upside down on the table. Each participant silently thanks his or her particular ancestor for participating in the ceremony and bids them farewell.

The rite is ended. Each participant is responsible for the food and drink offered to his or her ancestor. The ancestor's meal may be taken home and set out ritually for them, or it may be offered to the spirits of the ancestors by pouring out the drink as a libation (outdoors) and burying the food. The pouring of the drink onto the ground and the burial of the food signify that the meal is being sent to the Underworld residence of the spirits of the ancestors. Be sure to dispose of the ancestor's meal in a reverent and responsible manner; throwing it in the trash does no honor to anyone. Perhaps a modern version of the burial of the ancestor's meal would be to add it to the compost pile, whence it will be 'reincarnated' in the garden, thus completing the cycle.

Bibliography

Adler, Margot. *Drawing Down the Moon*. Boston: Beacon Press, 1981.

Amargi: Interdisciplinary Journal of the Ecosophical Research Association. Vol. 1, no. 2 (Nov. 1, 1988); Vol. II, no. 5 (Feb. 1, 1990); Vol. III, no. 6 (May 1, 1990).

Angus, S. *The Mystery-Religions: A Study in the Religious Background of Early Christianity*. 1928, rpt. New York: Dover Publications, 1975.

Bachofen, J.J. *Myth, Religion and Mother Right*. Princeton: Princeton University Press, 1967.

Beard, Mary R. *Woman as Force in History*. London: Collier-Macmillan, 1946.

Betancourt, Philip P. *The History of Minoan Pottery*. Princeton, NJ: Princeton University Press, 1985.

Biers, William R. *The Archaeology of Greece: An Introduction*. Ithaca, NY: Cornell University Press, 1987.

Boulding, Elise. *The Underside of History*. Boulder, Colorado: Westview Press, 1976.

Bulfinch, Thomas. *Bulfinch's Mythology: The Age of Fable*. Garden City, New York: Doubleday and Company, Inc., 1968.

Campbell, Joseph. *The Hero With a Thousand Faces*. Bollinger Series. Princeton: Princeton University Press, 1973.

Campbell, Joseph. *The Masks of God*. Vol. I-IV. New York: Penguin Books, 1977.

Campbell, Joseph. *Myths to Live By*. New York: Penguin Books, 1972.

Campbell, Joseph. *Primitive Mythology*. New York: Penguin Books, 1985.

Castleden, Rodney. *Minoans: Life in Bronze Age Crete*. London: Routledge, 1993.

Chadwick, John. *The Decipherment of Linear B*. Cambridge:

Cambridge University Press, 1998.

Chadwick, John. *Reading the Past: Linear B and Related Scripts.* Berkeley and Los Angeles: University of California Press, 1997.

Cooper, J.C. *The Aquarian Dictionary of Festivals.* Northamptonshire, England: The Aquarian Press, 1990.

Cottrell, Leonard. *The Bull of Minos.* New York: Holt, Rinehart and Winston, 1965.

d'Alviella, Count Goblet. *The Migration of Symbols.* New York: University Books, 1956.

de Selincourt, Aubrey. *The World of Herodotus.* Boston: Little, Brown and Company, 1962.

Durdin-Robertson, Lawrence. *The Symbolism of Temple Architecture.* Enniscorthy, County Wexford, United Kingdom: Cesara Publications, 1978.

Eisler, Riane. *The Chalice and the Blade: Our History, Our Future.* San Francisco: HarperCollins Publishers, 1988.

Eisler, Riane and David Love. *The Partnership Way: New Tools for Living and Learning: A Practical Companion for The Chalice and The Blade in Our Lives, Our Communities, and Our World.* San Francisco: HarperCollins Publishers, 1990.

Eliade, Mircea. *Patterns in Comparative Religion.* Sheed & Ward, 1958.

Eliade, Mircea. *Rites and Symbols of Initiation.* New York: Harper & Row, 1958.

Farrar, Janet and Stewart. *The Witches' Goddess: The Feminine Principle of Divinity.* Custer, Washington: Phoenix Publishing, Inc., 1987.

Feyerabend, Dr. Karl. *Langenscheidt's Pocket Greek Dictionary.* New York: Langenscheidt Publishers, Inc.

Frazer, Sir James George. *The Golden Bough: A Study in Magic and Religion.* New York: The Macmillan Company, Abridged Edition, 1951.

Freely, John. *Crete.* New York: New Amsterdam Books, 1988.

Friedrich, Walter L. *Fire in the Sea: The Santorini Volcano: Natural History and the Legend of Atlantis*. Cambridge: Cambridge University Press, 2000.

Gimbutas, Marija. *The Goddesses and Gods of Old Europe: Myths and Cult Images*. Berkeley: University of California Press, 1974.

Graham, James Walter. *The Palaces of Crete*. Princeton, NJ: Princeton University Press, 1987.

Graves, Robert. *The White Goddess: A Historical Grammar of Poetic Myth*. USA: Farrar Straus and Cudahy, Inc., 1948.

Guthrie, W.K.C. *The Greeks and Their Gods*. Boston: Beacon Press, 1955.

Hamilton, Edith. *Mythology*. New York: The New American Library, Mentor Edition, 1969.

Herm, Gerhard. Trans. Caroline Hillier. *The Phoenicians: The Purple Empire of the Ancient World*. 1973, rpt. and trans. New York: William Morrow and Company, Inc. 1975.

Higgins, Reynold. *The Archaeology of Minoan Crete*. New York: Henry Z. Walck, Inc., 1973.

Higgins, Reynold. *Minoan and Mycenaean Art*. London: Thames & Hudson, 1997.

Huxley, Francis. *The Dragon: Nature of Spirit, Spirit of Nature*. London: Thames and Hudson, Ltd., 1979.

Jung, Carl G. *Man and His Symbols*. New York: Doubleday & Co., 1964.

Konsola, Dora. Trans. Alexandra Doumas. *Crete: Knossos, Phaistos, Aghia Triada, Gortyn, Malia, Zakros, Gournia, Herakleion Museum, Aghias Nikolaos Museum, Chania Museum*. Athens: John Decopoulos, 1983.

Leach, Maria, ed. *Standard Dictionary of Folklore, Mythology, and Legend*. New York: Funk & Wagnalls Co., 1950.

Leeming, David Adams. *The World of Myth*. New York: Oxford University Press, 1990.

Lloyd, Seton, Hans Wolfgang Muller and Roland Martin. *Ancient Architecture: Mesopotamia, Egypt, Crete, Greece*. New York:

Harry N. Abrams, 1974.

Mackenzie, Donald A. *Crete & Pre-Hellenic Myths and Legends*. London: Studio Editions Ltd., 1995.

Marinatos, Nanno. *Minoan Kingship and the Solar Goddess: A Near Eastern Koine*. Champaign: University of Illinois Press, 2010.

Marinatos, Nanno. *Minoan Religion: Ritual, Image, and Symbol*. Columbia, South Carolina: University of South Carolina Press, 1993.

Martin, Roland. *Greek Architecture*. London: Phaidon Press/Electa, 2004.

McEnroe, John C. *Architecture of Minoan Crete: Constructing Identity in the Aegean Bronze Age*. Austin: University of Texas Press, 2010.

Monaghan, Patricia. *Book of Goddesses and Heroines*. New York: Dutton, 1981.

Morgan, Lyvia. *The Miniature Wall Paintings of Thera: A Study in Aegean Culture and Iconography*. Cambridge, UK: Cambridge University Press, 1988.

Murray, Alexander S. *Who's Who in Mythology: A Classic Guide to the Ancient World*, 2nd edition. 1874, rpt. New York: Bonanza Books, 1988.

Murray, Gilbert. *Five Stages of Greek Religion*. Garden City, New York: Doubleday and Company, Inc., Anchor Edition, 1955.

Nilsson, M.P. *Minoan-Mycenaean Religion*. Cambridge University Press, 1950.

Nilsson, M.P. *The Mycenaean Origin of Greek Mythology*. Cambridge University Press, 1932.

O'Brien, Cormac. *The Fall of Empires: From Glory to Ruin, an Epic Account of History's Ancient Civilizations*. New York: Fall River Press, 2009.

Pennick, Nigel. *Magical Alphabets*. York Beach, Maine: Samuel Weiser, Inc., 1992.

Pomeroy, Sarah B. *Goddesses, Whores, Wives, and Slaves: Women in Classical Antiquity*. New York: Schocken Books, 1975.

Sjoo, Monica, and Mor, Barbara. *The Great Cosmic Mother: Rediscovering the Religion of the Earth*. San Francisco: Harper & Row, 1987.

Stone, Merlin. *When God Was a Woman*. New York: Prentice Hall Press, 1982.

Swann, Thomas Burnett. *Cry Silver Bells*. New York: Daw Books, Inc., 1977.

Swann, Thomas Burnett. *Day of the Minotauros*. New York: Ace Books, Inc., 1966.

Vandenberg, Philipp. *The Mystery of the Oracles*. New York: Macmillan Publishing Co., Inc.

Vaughan, Agnes Carr. *The House of the Double Axe: The Palace at Knossos*. Garden City, New York: Doubleday and Company, Inc., 1959.

Walker, Barbara G. *The Woman's Dictionary of Symbols and Sacred Objects*. San Francisco: Harper Collins Publishers, 1988.

Walker, Barbara G. *The Woman's Encyclopedia of Myths and Secrets*. San Francisco: Harper Collins Publishers, 1983.

Warren, Peter. *The Aegean Civilizations*. New York: Peter Bedrick Books, 1989.

Watkins, Calvert, ed. *The American Heritage Dictionary of Indo-European Roots*. Boston: Houghton Mifflin Company, 1985.

Wunderlich, Hans Georg. Trans. Richard Winston. *The Secret of Crete*. Athens: 1983.

Index

Moon Books invites you to begin or deepen your encounter with Paganism, in all its rich, creative, flourishing forms.